Praise for

PRAY LIKE A GOURMET

"Simply beautiful! David Brazzeal takes the hospitality traditions of the French and the Brazilians and stirs in spiritual disciplines and alternative worship practices for a book on prayer unlike anything you've read before. He reminds us that time with God is a rich and delicious banquet that we share together, and not a drive-thru fast food meal we eat alone."
Michael Frost, Morling College, Sydney, Australia

"From the moment you read the table of contents, *Pray Like A Gourmet* becomes a banquet for the soul and spirit. Since when has prayer been such a mouth-watering, taste bud-awakening experience? There's no room for deprivation here. Come and most heartily feast!"
Pierre LeBel, teacher and author of *Imago Dei*; YWAM Leader in Canada

"David Brazzeal takes the simplicity of gospel and makes it come alive in a most imaginative way. Using metaphors of food, he leads the reader through practices of prayer and time with God that enrich our relationship with the Father."
Chris Julian, university campus minister in Rio Grande du Sul, Brazil

"I learned about new tools and tantalizing ingredients to add to the shelves of my prayer closet, ones I have never sampled before. For each prayer form, he provides creative, embodied ways to practice them. He is both a playful host and a serious chef at this delicious banquet. This is a book to use over and over again."
Sybil MacBeth, author of *Praying in Color: Drawing a New Path to God*

"We all get stuck in prayer—eating from the same old menu over and over. If your prayer life has grown bland and tasteless, you definitely need to read this menu. It will take you to a new level of praying, whetting your appetite to pray more deeply, enriching your life to live more freely and fully in Christ."
Randy Rains, Associate Vice President for Spiritual Life & Formation, International Mission Board, SBC, Richmond, Virginia

'PRAY LIKE A GOURMET

CREATIVE WAYS TO FEED YOUR SOUL

David Brazzeal

ACTIVE
PRAYER
SERIES

Illustrations by Willemijn de Groot

PARACLETE PRESS
BREWSTER, MASSACHUSETTS

2015 First Printing

Pray Like a Gourmet: Creative Ways to Feed Your Soul

Copyright © 2015 by David Brazzeal

ISBN 978-1-61261-627-8

Illustrations by Willemijn de Groot
www.willemijndegroot.nl

Library of Congress Cataloging-in-Publication Data
Brazzeal, David.
  Pray like a gourmet : creative ways to feed your soul / David Brazzeal.
    pages cm. — (Active prayer series)
  ISBN 978-1-61261-627-8
  1. Prayer—Christianity. 2. Dinners and dining—Religious aspects—Christianity. I. Title.
  BV210.3.B736 2015
  248.3›2—dc23   2014044485

10 9 8 7 6 5 4 3 2 1

Published by Paraclete Press
Brewster, Massachusetts
www.paracletepress.com
Printed in the United States of America

*To my kind and gentle wife Sanan,
my friend and companion all along this journey.*

CONTENTS

Part
ONE

Part

ONE

Pull up a chair. Take a taste. Come join us.
Life is so endlessly delicious.

— RUTH REICHL

"Teach Your Children Well" (Gourmet Magazine, 2007)

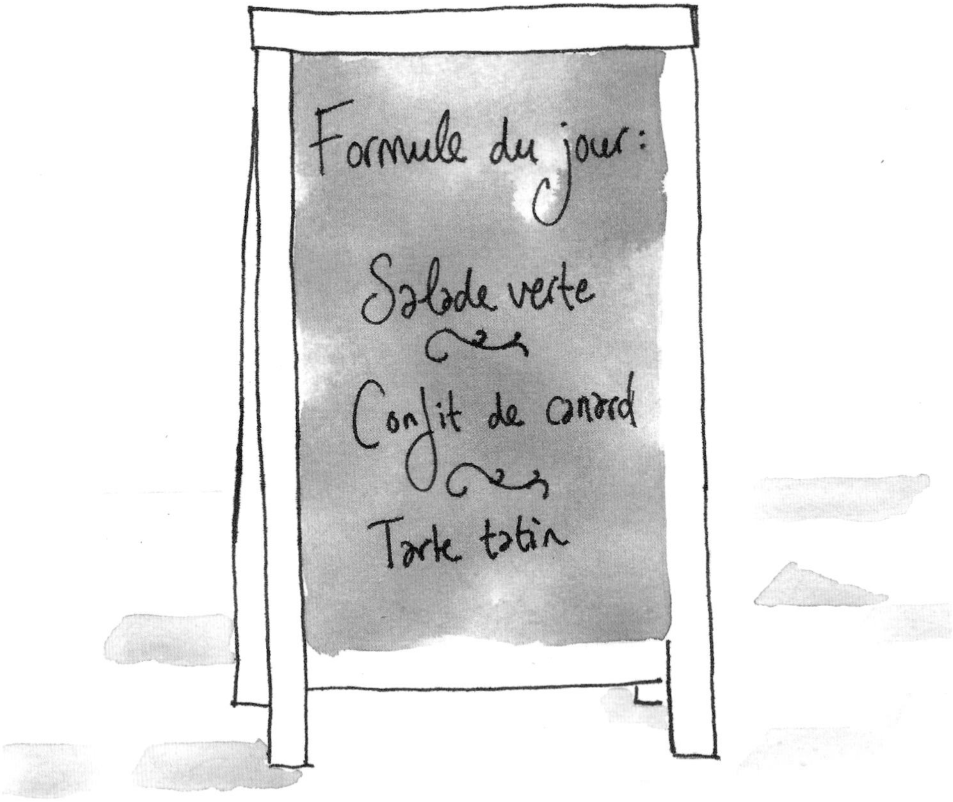
Formule du jour:
Salade verte
Confit de canard
Tarte tatin

Chapter 1

WHETTING YOUR APPETITE

I had my first French meal and I never got over it.
It was just marvelous. We had oysters and a lovely dry white wine.
And then we had one of those lovely scalloped dishes and the lovely,
creamery buttery sauce. Then we had a roast duck
and I don't know what else.

—JULIA CHILD, *Larry King Live, CNN*, aired 8.21.2004, transcript.[1]

 ome with me to the heart of Paris. A dear friend has invited us over for dinner tonight. It promises to be a particularly scrumptious affair. I'm following my usual checklist for such an evening:

- Verify arrival time : 20h00 ✔
- Buy flowers @ the street market ✔
- Locate apartment on GPS ✔
- Determine best metro route ✔
- Dress nicely ✔
- Leave for the soireé : 19h30. ✔

On the metro my mouth begins watering as I imagine the *possibilités culinaires* just ahead.

(20h30) The evening gets started with an *apéro* (appetizer) and drinks. Sweet wine from our host's particular region in France is offered along with dried sausage and *pâté*.

(21h00) Everyone is now seated. A colorful *salade* first appears on the table, almost enough for an entire meal. But take it easy . . . remember there's more to come.

(21h30) Salad is followed by a simple *soupe* or *purée*. And of course, a *baguette*. This is followed by a lengthy pause in the eating in order to enhance the conversation . . . long enough to make the inexperienced wonder if the meal is finished.

(22h30) The *pièce de résistance* (main dish) makes its appearance now accompanied by an interesting vegetable dish or two. *Boeuf bourguignon* maybe. *Confit de canard*. There is a paired wine, of course, and a slice of *foie gras* on the side.

(23h20) A cutting board with a number of cheeses appears: perhaps a *Camembert*, a *Comté*, a *Cantal*, some *chèvre* (goat cheese), and a *Roquefort*. With yet another baguette. Another wine.

(23h50) Dessert is served and enjoyed: *Crème brûlée peut-être* or *Mousse au chocolat?*

(00h10) Coffee orders are taken. I'll have a small espresso. Since it is so late in the evening, would you prefer *déca* (decaffeinated)?

LES POSSIBILITÉS

Since moving to France, I have experienced a wonderful change in the meaning of "We'd like to invite you over for a meal at our place." It has expanded. Lengthened. Upscaled in quality, in taste, in smell, in appearance . . . and I am loving it!

Even if you don't live in Paris, for most of us in the world's developed countries, eating has become potentially an amazing experience. Never before in history have we had access to such a variety of food or so many ways to prepare it. There are seemingly infinite places to access it and infinite genres of entertainment associated with consuming it. The choices are absolutely stunning— cuisine from every corner of the globe, fusion versions of almost everything, reality cooking shows—oops, strike that—there are entire cooking *networks* now, searchable online recipe sites, gourmet food magazines, theme restaurants for the whole family, exotic culinary vacations on clipper ships, endless user reviews and recommendations, food forums, and chat rooms. In addition, there are numerous global food *movements*: fair trade, organic, slow, local, vegetarian and vegan, kosher and halal, just to name a few.

Still, despite all these first-time-in-history resources in the culinary world, many people even in the most developed countries still exist on uninteresting, unvarying, and impoverished diets.

THREE TELLING TALES

Tale #1: After attending a winter conference in Alberta, I caught a ride back to Calgary with a professor friend and his wife. Before leaving the mountainous region, they asked if I would be up for stopping for a quick lunch at Wendy's.

"No problemo. Sounds good," was my response. Since it was past noon, most of the skiers were on the slopes. Lines were short. My friends seemed to know what they wanted to order, and so did I.

"Do you order that salad often?" my friend's wife asked me.

"No. First time . . . thought I'd try a different salad," I answered.

My friend exclaimed with a chuckle, "You are *so* right-brained . . . I really like that about you!"

"What? What's so right-brained about that?"

"Well, we actually have a habit of eating at Wendy's every day for lunch," the wife sheepishly confessed. "And . . . we order the same thing every time."

Tale #2: My wife and I were taking some extended time off to be near two of our daughters in Savannah, Georgia. The city is known for its massive oak trees laced with Spanish moss, historic antebellum homes, and especially its Southern cuisine. We'd been there just long enough to discover some great little local restaurants to recommend when a friend contacted us about coming through town.

"Hey Dave, we'll be passing through Savannah on the way to Florida for our family vacation. Maybe we could all have a meal together? I see on the Internet that there's a Golden Corral in Savannah. Our family loves those cheap all-you-can-eat buffets. What d'ya think?"

"Hmmm . . . not my first (second or third) choice but okay, if that's what you like."

Tale #3: In Montréal, Québec, I had a comic book artist friend— probably the wildest and craziest friend I've ever had. (Yes, you, Paul.) In almost every area of life, he is adventurous, improvisational, and over-the-top. His clothes are extremely colorful. His entrance into a room of friends will typically be accompanied with arms raised and a yell of some sort. His self-created comic world is practically as real to him as I am. He is wild and crazy, *except* when it comes to food. He eats *exclusively* hamburgers, hot dogs, french fries, and pizza with only an occasional (but very reluctant) edible exception when invited out.

One night at a party Paul confessed, "Hey guys! I've got a problem. My in-laws sent me fifty dollars and told me to go somewhere nice to eat with my wife."

"Why is that a problem?" several of us asked simultaneously.

"Well, all the places I like to eat, you know, they're only pizza and hot dog joints. There's no way I could possibly spend that much money at places like that for just the two of us."[2]

7

Do these tales sound at all familiar? If not about food in your life, then are they reminiscent of your *spiritual diet*? Is there something in your spirit that keeps telling you it should be different: more interesting, more engaging, more creative, more profound? Does your prayer life feel like you're eating the same food over and over every day—mixing the same ingredients but hoping for a new, more enticing dish?

Or perhaps you're experiencing something more like a divine drive-thru. You hurriedly place "your order," always in a rush, expecting God to deliver it promptly at the next window?

Maybe your most intimate moments with God are akin to grabbing a cheap frozen dinner from the stack in the freezer and tossing it in the microwave: bland, monotonous, and predictably uninteresting.

8

I understand. I've been there too. We all deal with twenty-first-century pressures, stresses, distractions, and time constraints. We fall prey to the default mode of our culture—fast and efficient. We've even allowed what George Ritzer calls the "McDonaldization"[3] of our society to invade and take root within the very relationship that is most precious to us—the one that, in fact, is the source that sustains and nurtures our soul. No wonder we feel spiritually anemic and malnourished.

In culinary circles around the world, many people are now pushing back and taking the time to peel, chop, and cook locally grown food with their own unique flair. We, too, can push back and engage in seeking authentic, calm, and refreshing nourishment for our soul—each one of us, of course, with our own flair.

It is my hope that this book will help move your spiritual life in that direction, that it will help to redefine "praying" for you in the same way that living in France has changed my definition of eating. May it expand your prayer palette so your soul becomes accustomed to new tastes and textures. May it invite you on the adventure of mastering ancient exotic recipes from yet unexplored realms of spiritual cuisine. May you learn the joy of creatively feeding your own soul. In other words, I invite you to pray like a gourmet!

Chapter 2

ACQUIRING A TASTE

I tasted you, and now I hunger and thirst for you.
—ST. AUGUSTINE OF HIPPO, *Confessions*

Go where your best prayers take you.
—FREDERICK BUECHNER, *Telling Secrets*

Step back in time with me . . . back to the late 1980s. Shoulder pads were thick. Music was cheesy. Synths were glassy. Glasses were big and hair was even bigger. Coat sleeves rolled up. Bracelets slapped on. "The Internet? What's that?"

I was in Brazil, in the amazing, exotic city of Rio de Janeiro. I lived in a two-story, white-stucco house on a quiet street that ran up the mountain range where the famous open-armed Christ statue stands. A tropical forest enveloped the end of our street. An occasional monkey appeared in the trees. The sound of a gurgling stream running behind our house provided a continuous sound track to life.

II

Living in the house with me was my wonderful, supportive wife, Sanan, and four fun, fabulous daughters. A maid ironed our clothes and cooked our lunches, which always included black beans and rice. Life was good.

I was in Brazil teaching gifted young composers how to put their ideas onto musical staff paper. I was editing music for a Christian publishing house and leading worship at a new Brazilian church near the Barra da Tijuca beach. I was studying the beautiful Portuguese language.

However, something was fundamentally wrong. My life felt like the moment in a movie when the whole family has gathered from afar to enjoy a wonderful Thanksgiving meal. The table is beautifully decorated; Grandma and Grandpa are both there; the grandkids are impeccably well dressed and well behaved; and a huge turkey is delivered to the table with fanfare and applause. Everyone takes their seats as Grandpa ceremoniously cuts into the turkey, placing a large slab of breast meat on each plate, already loaded with other delicacies. Then the family digs into the feast . . . but one by one they quietly discover that the beautiful turkey is . . . well . . . incredibly dry . . . and . . . (slight cough) tasteless.

That was my life at the time. On the surface, all was well . . . everything was going great; but inside I felt something like that turkey, incredibly dry . . . *seco demais*, as I had learned to say in Portuguese.

HUNGER STRIKE

Why did I feel so empty inside? After all, I was actively participating in a good church. I was praying, reading the Bible, helping people, leading people in worship, and expanding the kingdom.

The answer to my frustration didn't come quickly. I pondered the problem with greater and greater frequency. I doubled down on all of the above good things. It didn't help. I only grew more frustrated. I got angry with God. Why was he doing this to me? Even with a loving wife and supportive colleagues, I felt like I couldn't confide in anyone; I mean which missionary colleague could I open up to and reveal such interior stagnation? I started to get desperate. I decided to quit eating. (I say it that way because I didn't feel spiritual enough to call the experience a fast. It was more like a hunger strike or even a temper tantrum against God.)

That's right, I decided to ball my life up into one big fist and more or less stick it in God's face to see what he would do about it. For the next few days my increasing frustration combined with my lack of physical nourishment powered the raw expressions of my "grievances" to the Almighty. Here's a sampler of what passed through the voice of my soul:

> Ok, look here, God. I'm really frustrated. Here's what's going to happen: I'm going to quit eating until you break through somehow and tell me what to do . . . you've got to somehow communicate to me.

> You are the one who has led me to this place but in doing so you've taken away all my sources of inspiration. I can no longer buy a new CD of music that touches my soul. Chuck Swindoll is no longer on my radio. Vince, my best friend who

always talked me through my problems, is no longer around. No new books to read. Sure, I go to church; but to be honest, I'm just not hearing you in this new language.

13

To my surprise, something began to seep into the cracks of my complaining. In the pauses, when I gave myself time to listen, other kinds of thoughts began echoing around . . . thoughts from another place . . . as if someone else was intentionally dropping them into my soul, like gentle, soothing responses to my raging rant. Then one of them became crystal clear:

So . . . seems like it's just you and me now.

What do you mean?

It seems like it's just YOU and ME now. I've actually been waiting awhile for this moment.

Really? I don't get it.

Wasn't this supposed to be a relationship? Just you and me . . . not a group project.

This little dialogue set up some serious self-reflection. I began to realize that I had been surviving on spiritual "feeding tubes"—just plugging myself in whenever and wherever I felt I could be "spiritually fed." But when I moved to another country, all those convenient tubes were yanked out in one fell swoop and left to dangle in midair. At the same time, my serious need for real spiritual nourishment was growing exponentially. I not only had new leadership responsibilities, but I had to do everything in another language and cultural context. Pile on top of that a growing family with stresses and needs of their own. So, no wonder I felt empty inside!

At this point, my hunger strike became a fast. The scene shifted from my soul being frustrated to being famished. I was getting somewhere, but I was by no means there yet. Dialog with God had been reestablished, and even though I didn't have all the answers, I was hungry for them.

> *Listen, God, I really want to figure this out! In fact, this is becoming more important to me than anything else. I'm getting really hungry!*
>
> *But if at the end of all of this I find out that this relationship is NOT a real possibility . . .that it really can't happen . . . then I'm going to quit everything.*
>
> *So, how does this work, REALLY? The stark reality is that YOU are invisible and YOU are silent. I am here and I can talk. How can this be a relationship? Will You PLEASE teach me how to do this?! I am not eating until you break through to me and tell me how this works.*

AN ANCIENT RECIPE

Several days into my fast, I had an unusual experience. A small, blue-ish book on my bookshelf seemed to grab my attention. I pulled it out and read the title: *Experiencing the Depths of Jesus Christ*. I thought to myself, *ugly graphics, monochrome cover, pretentious title. Can't be good.* I slid it back. But then the book seemed to challenge me from the shelf: *I dare you to read me!*

I pulled it back out and thumbed through the initial pages searching for more ammunition . . . or excuses. *Look . . . first published in 1685? Sorry, I'm not reading anything that archaic. Written by Madame Guyon . . . who in the world!*

*Isn't my title what you're seeking . . .
Depth? Jesus Christ? Experience?*

I gave in and started reading.

It took awhile to adjust to the antiquated language, but by chapter two I realized this book was telling me exactly what I was literally starving to know—what to do when I'm alone with God.

> Turn to the Scripture; choose some passage that is simple and fairly practical. Next, come to the Lord. Come quietly and humbly. There, before Him, read a small portion of the passage of Scripture you have opened to. Be careful as you read. Take in fully, gently and carefully what you are reading. Taste it and digest it as you read.

"Taste it"? "Digest it"? This is good stuff.

16

As you read, pause. The pause should be quite gentle. You have paused so that you may set your mind on the Spirit. You have set your mind inwardly on Christ. . . . The Lord is found only within your spirit, in the recesses of your being, in the Holy of Holies; this is where He dwells. The Lord will meet you in your spirit. It was Augustine who once said that he had lost much time in the beginning of his Christian experience by trying to find the Lord outwardly rather than by turning inwardly.[4]

I've never heard this before! why has no one ever explained this to me?

I devoured the first few chapters of Madame Guyon's book and at the same time I began eating again. God had broken through to me and given me more than just a big bone to chew on—this was meaty stuff. Not just a book I could breeze through and lay aside, it was giving me something to diligently work on, a spiritual skill to perfect.

As I look back, that was my first "cooking lesson." **And** I really liked the taste of the entrée. In fact, I liked it so much that I decided to keep it to myself . . . make it my very own secret recipe and not tell anyone. Well, I told my wife, but no one else! You see, since I had never heard of this French Catholic woman and her place in church history, and since no pastor had ever taught me to pray like this, the last thing I wanted was some well-meaning colleague to throw water on my campfire by saying something like "Don't tell me you've fallen for that heresy!" Only later did I receive surprisingly clear confirmation that I was indeed going in the right direction, but that's another story.

17

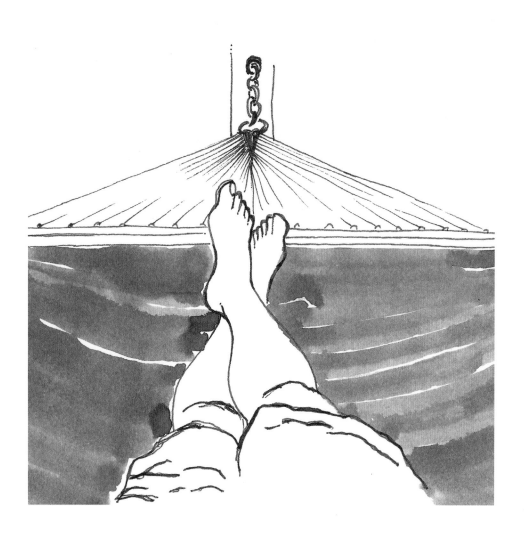

Chapter 3

BECOMING A CHEF

Most of our life is spent starving at a well laid table
because we don't know how to use the gifts that we've received.
— THOMAS KEATING, *The Gift of Life: Death & Dying (video)*

MID-AIR KITCHEN

Just as the taste of simple food is utterly delectable after a long fast, so was this simple new spiritual practice. But I found myself hungry for even more.

It was about this time when I discovered the importance of the small outdoor veranda upstairs at the back of our house. A stream ran below it, an avocado tree hung over it, and beyond it was the urban tropical forest that led up to Corcovado Mountain. Another great thing about the veranda, though, was its strong, built-in hammock hooks. I bought a simple red-plaid hammock and began spending time in it.

There I lay, suspended between heaven and earth, a powerful physical image for the spiritual place where I felt I somehow belonged. I practiced reading small portions of Scripture, meditating on the words, slowly tasting and digesting them. The veranda was becoming my sacred space and the hammock, a sacred object. If my hammock

20

ever ripped from overuse or staying out in the rain, I felt compelled to stop everything and go buy another one immediately.

As I lay there, wanting to spend more time with God but not really knowing what to do, I began to experiment. I suppose it could have been out of boredom, but I really had nothing to lose. I imagined I was holding a clean but totally empty frying pan and I didn't know what to put in it. There was no one around to impress. God would be the only one joining me for dinner. Since he *is* invisible and really doesn't talk much, I suppose I began talking to myself. What if I spent most of my time at this meal just praising him? What would that be like? How would I do that? Maybe this was my "wild and crazy" chef phase, just throwing any old ingredients into the pan and turning the heat up; but we all have to start somewhere.

I think most of us bring to cooking an acquired sense of which ingredients combine especially well and which do not. All of us *do* have our own eating experiences to draw upon. The challenge is to draw on the past but not be bound by it. It's really not that hard to create a new dish based on what we've already tasted or experienced. Here is a starting-point prayer exercise: start by simply telling God how great and wonderful he is. Use lots of adjectives as ingredients. Explore the well-stocked spice rack of his intriguing and sometimes exotic names. Also, be encouraged that many others in the past have cooked up the same or similar dishes. Feel free to borrow some of their words and ideas from their recipes.

I remember the day when I discovered that a master chef from the past had cooked up a very similar recipe to the one I was testing. I don't remember the exact book, but it closed with a prayer by St. Francis of Assisi, similar to this one:

You are holy, Lord, the only God,
and Your deeds are wonderful.
You are strong.
You are great.
You are the Most High.
You are Almighty.
You, Holy Father are King of heaven and earth.
You are Three and One, Lord God, all Good.
You are Good, all Good, supreme Good,
Lord God, living and true.
You are love. You are wisdom.
You are humility. You are endurance.
You are rest. You are peace.
You are joy and gladness.
You are justice and moderation.
You are all our riches, and You suffice for us.
You are beauty.
You are gentleness.
You are our protector.
You are our guardian and defender.
You are our courage. You are our haven and our hope.
You are our faith, our great consolation.
You are our eternal life, Great and Wonderful Lord,
God Almighty, Merciful Savior.[5]

It is hard to relate how incredibly encouraging this was to me. I recognized it immediately as a spontaneous praise eruption from an ancient source with many of the same ingredients I was using—random nouns, names, and adjectives, but all with a consistent, repetitive sentence structure. I had stirred up a very similar dish to

22

St. Francis of Assisi's without knowing it! This helped assure me that I wasn't crazy. It meant my intuitive, trial-and-error cooking experiments were leading me in the right direction. It meant Francis had created this same kind of spiritual space. He prayed the same way I did, but eight centuries earlier! *Hmmm . . . I wonder if he had a hammock?*

These early experiments were wonderful! Soon, I even became more poetic with my words. Then it was time to throw something else in the pan. *Could I praise God without words? What would that look like?* I started singing, inventing new melodies simply based on "Alleluia" and other phrases from Scripture. I tried drawing and sketching.

I had this wild idea—*What if I asked God how he wanted me to praise him today?* That was when things really started to get interesting! I began to have these slight impressions of his responses. One day it would be some-

thing like, Today, lie down prostrate, face to the ground, don't say a word, just feel my awesomeness. or another day—Dance for me, Dave . . . another David once danced for me and I loved it. or—Read to me of my greatness, as much as you can, as expressively as you can.

This same process began to ooze into the other forms of prayer I was trying out in those early days: thanksgiving, confession, intercession. *Show me a new way to thank you today. Give me a handle on how to pray for this situation. Is it possible to make confession fun?* The resulting experiments weren't very organized or consistent, but they were all good. It was as if God had become not only the object of my praise and thanksgiving but my creative partner as well. Before knowing how to label it, I was discovering some very important secrets of spiritual cookery straight from the Master Chef.

Simultaneously, I came across in my reading what to me were key pieces of information. These applied directly to the systematic workings of the spiritual-creative interplay. They helped explain and support what was going on within me.

The first was the simple idea that imagination is a good thing— actually a gift of God to be used and applied to my spiritual life. This came my way through Richard Foster's classic work *A Celebration of Discipline*.[6] It seems I had heard during most of my teenage years to be suspicious of my imagination, to not let it run too wild, to keep it in check. The reason was never very specific but always hinted toward lust and potential sexual sin.

Then I came across a second piece of information somewhere, maybe in that old edition of *Mysticism*[7] by Evelyn Underhill I found in the attic of a Brazilian theological library. It made the point that creativity and spirituality function on the same side of the brain. If that is true, it is quite reasonable and natural for them to function together. The prophets and mystics were obviously aware of this connection.

The third tidbit came from Peter Lord's *Hearing God*.[8] It took the mystery out of the way God speaks to us by simply stating that God speaks by planting ideas in our mind. More precisely, when we create an environment where our spirit is in sync with the Divine Spirit, then we should be on the lookout for good, positive, helpful thoughts and ideas from a source beyond ourselves.

Once I mixed all these things together, I realized there *really is* a natural interplay between my spirituality and my creativity. When I enter into a spirit of prayer, I can cultivate a receptive space and actually ask God for creative ideas that will enhance my praying. Then, these creative practices allow me to enter into the spiritual space even more quickly and deeply. The result is a spiraling effect leading to ever-expanding dimensions, encompassing both deeper spirituality and heightened creativity.

23

PARIS — Place de la Bastille.

It has now been more than twenty-five years since those days in the Brazilian hammock. I've moved around a bit since then—from the cool waterfalls and black sand beaches of Guadeloupe to Montréal's nose-numbing cold and its great summer festivals. I've traded my hammock in for an assortment of other sacred spaces—various-sized rooms, certain comfortable chairs or beds, parks, forests, and occasionally the public labyrinths I enjoy creating. These days, God and I most often cook things up on a used IKEA couch in an old Parisian apartment with the creakiest floors you've ever heard.

By the way: Ironically, I now live just a couple of blocks from the Bastille in Paris. For over seven years, Madame Guyon was imprisoned there for the radical ideas she wrote about in that little book, the one that beckoned me and began changing my ideas on, and practice of, prayer forever. Seeing the Bastille daily keeps me anchored to those early days of renewal and discovery. I often read Guyon's quotes to visiting friends as we stand in the place now marked with inlaid bricks in the street and sidewalk where that ominous medieval castle, her prison, once stood.

Not only have I moved on geographically from where this story began, but I've moved on ecclesiastically as well. I'm no longer a worship leader in a traditional church, but I've helped start four new innovative churches, each one unique.

I've also learned the proper terminology for what I went through in Rio. Some would call it the "dark night of the soul."[9] I've been able to follow the stories of the mystics enough to realize that we share a common journey. Yes, it seems to sometimes be God's modus operandi— to drag us into periods of dryness or darkness, where he "appears" to not be present. It is the very longing that we develop in those times that allows, leads, inspires, compels us to move to the next level.

I continue to consistently invite God in when I hear him knocking. Often I need to knock on his door as well. We've had many, many wonderful meals together. The courses have varied, new ones have been added, and different ones have taken priority at different times. New creative recipes have been developed, but some of the classics still remain as go-to favorites.

Now, I invite you to join me in setting up a basic kitchen with God. That is what we will continue to explore in Part One. Then, in Part Two, we will discover practical recipes for cooking up your own spiritual feast. *Bon appétit!*

25

Chapter 4

SPREADING THE TABLE

Love came a guest
Within my breast,
My soul was spread,
Love banqueted.
—IBN HAZM, *The Ring of the Dove*

FOOD:
THE METAPHOR OF CHOICE

T his book is not the first to play with metaphors linking *haute cuisine* and the *Haute Divine*. It follows a very long tradition. You may recall that the Bible actually opens with a story about a simple piece of fruit and how it led to some serious spiritual problems for us humans. Later on, ancient Judaism was largely fashioned around a network of feasts and celebrations, often around a table of food delicacies to represent specific spiritual realities. And when choosing a way for his disciples to remember him after his impending death, Jesus flowed along in the Jewish Passover culinary tradition and served up a very simple meal of bread and wine—both of which, as you should remember, were and still are quite metaphorically charged.

In Jesus's creative storytelling, he used a banquet as a metaphor to illustrate the kingdom of God. In typical Jesus fashion, though, he turned the thing on its head by *not* describing a proper banquet with all the respectable guests who deserved to be there. No, the verbal picture he painted of the kingdom of God was a lavish banquet hall filled to overflowing with the total rejects of society: the poor, the handicapped, the rednecks, the immigrants, the street people, the bag ladies, the junkies, the prostitutes, the gays, the hoodies, the nobodies—one real crazy, wild party, if you ask me! (See Luke 14:12-23.)

Oh yes, and then there was also Jesus's little habit of feeding several thousand people in a single afternoon,[10] which I think was his way of saying, "I really wish I could sit down with each of you one-on-one over a nice meal; but since that is physically impossible right now, I will at least create one huge feast and share it with all of you." It is as if the food became a symbol of his nourishing presence among them just as it does today when believers observe Communion together.

Several religions practice specific food restrictions or fasting as spiritual reminders: Muslims have a month of fasting from dawn to sunset called Ramadan; many Buddhists and Hindus are vegetarians; Jews abstain from pork as well as from mixing meat and milk, just to mention a few of the worldwide practices.

Abstaining from physical food can play a powerful role in creating a hunger and receptivity for spiritual food (as I have personally experienced); but in other significant spots in the Bible, an intimate meal becomes the metaphor for a rendezvous with the Divine One. Consider the stories told in these three portions of Scripture.

THE FIRST BOOK

In the eighteenth chapter of Genesis, there's a rather strange story of God appearing to Abraham while he was sitting under the great trees of Mamre. The story is unusual because God appears in the form of three men. *(Hmmm . . . Trinity?)* Fortunately, Abraham recognizes him/them and immediately goes into host mode, inviting them to join him and Sarah for a meal. We all know what it's like to have guests show up unannounced, but what if it were God times three? Can you say *frantic*?

Luckily for Abraham and Sarah, this story took place a few millennia ago, when the pace of life was a good bit slower. Also, I think it helped that they were in the middle of a desert so there wasn't anywhere else to run off to for other options. As it turns out, Sarah even had time to make bread from scratch. Abraham told her to use the "finest flour" (*You know, Honey, the good stuff we keep to the side just in case God shows up for a meal someday.*) This meant Sarah took the time to mix the dough, knead it, let it rise a bit, and then bake it. Meanwhile, the servants wrestled down the best sheep in the herd, butchered it, built a fire, and roasted it. Now add to that a few jugs of goat-milk yogurt, and you have yourself a very tasty three-course meal. Then, just as they are all enjoying the food and each other's company, God drops on them the hugely important and beyond-imaginable news that Sarah is going to have a baby even though she's ninety years old. WOW! What a reason to celebrate!

The take away?

- God can show up unannounced for a meal with you.
- He may not look the way you think he should look.
- You should already be learning how to prepare that meal.
- The meal should be your best stuff.
- God may tell you something very important during his visit.

THE MIDDLE BOOK

As a kid, I was taught that if you open the Bible in the middle you'd probably land on the book of Psalms. And near the middle of everyone's favorite Psalm, the 23rd, there's this line: "You prepare a table before me in the presence of my enemies." I don't know how many times I've read or recited this Psalm without pondering what that line actually means, but here's my take on it. When things are a bit tense, when life is not going at its best, when the potential for disaster is just around the corner, when your enemies are all around you—and even staring you down!—that's when God lays out the red-checkered picnic cloth and says, "Oooo, this is a nice place. Let's hang out here together for a while . . . just you and me."

The take away?

- Once again, God shows up when you least expect it.
- He knows that when life gets chaotic, that's when you need him the most.
- God gently reaffirms his love in the midst of trying circumstances.

THE LAST BOOK

In the third chapter of the book of Revelation is another often-cited passage. It portrays God standing at the door of your life, calling for you and knocking on your door. It goes on to say that if anyone hears his voice and opens the door, then he will come in and they will *dine* together. We usually focus on the "opening the door" part of this verse, but I'd like to draw your attention to what happens *after* the door is opened. The verse is actually written to specifically highlight the reciprocity of the relationship: "I will come in and eat with them and they with me."

The take away?

- Hey! There he is again, showing up unannounced—definitely becoming a trend.
- God obviously *wants* this meal: he calls out to us and knocks on the door.
- But he doesn't barge in. He waits patiently for us to respond.
- The meal is mutually beneficial. Evidently, God enjoys this time as much as we do.

Don't take this meal-metaphor thing for granted. He could have included a number of other activities here:

I will come in and teach you great things.

I will come in and use your life in mighty ways.

I will come in and make everything go right for you.

I will come in and humiliate you and put you in your proper place.

I will come in and find out about all your deep, dark, dirty sins.

But, he didn't! He said that we would simply share a meal together. Mutual respect. Mutual vulnerability. Mutual nourishment. Mutual enjoyment. Beautiful, isn't it?

Think for a moment how this shapes your mental image of what God is like. Please, please throw away that bad picture of the angry old man in the sky just waiting to catch you doing something wrong. Throw it away for good! The great and glorious God, the Creator of all that ever was and ever will be, finds your address, shows up unannounced, waits for you to get ready—all for what? Because he wants to sit down and have a lovely meal together with you, just you and him. But why? Maybe he knows that if you do it once, you'll want to do it again . . . and then again and again. Ever notice that when people spend a lot of time together, they become like each other? Bottom line: Dining with God will slowly change your life.

Unless . . . you blow it!

But how could you blow such a sweet deal? Believe me, it's possible.

First of all, if you *never* open the door—*c'est fini*! You blow it. If you can't step up and take the risk to see what's behind Door Number One . . . well, then you'll never even know what you've missed, right?

You could also blow it if you open the door . . . but, well . . . I don't know . . . you just . . . how do I say . . . don't feel . . . well . . . worthy enough . . . to have a meal . . . with such a magnificent God. I've certainly been there! If this is you, then stop right now and re-read that part a few pages back about the huge banquet of rejects. He invites us *all* to the table! Even the most unworthy, the most awkward, the most insecure among us. And! He knows how to shape the experience to make it work for each of us. It's as if he already knows the cuisine we prefer and the kind of bistros we love.

You could also blow it if you do open the door but never really let the banquet happen because you limit the meal to fast food, junk food, or processed food. I think this is where a lot of us are stuck.

- Fast food . . . when we never take the time necessary to let the relationship develop.
- Junk food . . . when there's often very little substance to our self-centered prayers.
- Processed food . . . when we restrict ourselves to devotional guides or prayers written by others.

Just as eating well physically takes some time and effort, so does eating well spiritually. That's what the rest of this book is about. I'll share some simple ideas about how to expand the number of courses to choose from when you sit down for that special time, as well as practical suggestions to make it more fun, engaging, creative, moving, and profound.

Chapter 5

MIXING IT UP

Why must people kneel down to pray?
If I really wanted to pray I'll tell you what I'd do.
I'd go out into a great big field all alone or in the deep, deep woods
and I'd look up into the sky—up—up—up—into that lovely blue sky
that looks as if there was no end to its blueness.
And then I'd just feel a prayer.
—L. M. MONTGOMERY, *Anne of Green Gables*

THE BASICS

efore we jump into specific prayer recipes, here are two essential questions that are usually front and center in my mind when I start to pray:

1. What kinds of prayer are possible?

2. What means of expression are possible?

The answers to the first question are some prayer types you are probably already aware of, as well as some that may be less familiar. When I was a teenger someone taught me to pray with the acronym ACTS:

ADORATION OR PRAISE

CONFESSION

THANKSGIVING

SUPPLICATION OR ASKING

Those four are definitely the classics. A good start, but with maturity, necessity, and perhaps some boredom, I've added:

OBSERVATION

INTERCESSION

MEDITATION

CONTEMPLATION

And in recent years I've added a few others:

BLESSING

LAMENTING

JOINING

These are possible courses of a spiritual feast. They provide a great palette to work with, but there are certainly other variations out there and even more yet to be discovered. Each of these prayer practices is different, sometimes only subtly so. Each one adds unique flavor and texture to the prayer experience. Depending on your mood, your circumstances, your needs, your spiritual climate, and other factors, the mix of the components you choose will change. Let them serve you. Some you will use quite often. Others, like good friends, are always there when you need them. You would rarely, if ever, include all of them in one experience.

Whatever you do to spend concentrated time with God and whenever you choose to do it, it's a good idea to first break the experience down into various courses, parts, components, practices, or whatever you want to call them. Pick a few elements to create the prayer experience you need. Then, just as with an elegant meal, slowly experience course after course after course—each one different—each one bathing and massaging your soul's palette in its own unique way.

The immediate benefit you will experience will be a fresh sense of variety and diversity in your prayer time. The secondary benefit will be that your prayers will become less egocentric and self-absorbed because most of the above courses focus on God himself or on others and that's a good thing.

38

Now that the various "courses" of praying are laid out before you, the answer to the second question involving possible means of expression comes into play. The idea here is to move far beyond your default mode of praying, which for many is the old bow-your-head and close-your-eyes routine. Through the years I've gathered quite a wide-ranging variety of alternative possibilities:

I can speak.

I can read.

I can shout.

I can be silent.

I can be still.

I can sit, stand, kneel, lay, move, jump, dance . . .

I can chant an ancient hymn or improvise a new song.

I can write prose or poetry.

I can sketch, draw, doodle, paint, collage . . .

I can use plain paper or textured paper or "virtually" no paper.

I can use a pencil or colored pens, or a calligraphy stylus and ink.

I can use a cheap or elegant notebook or even make my own.

I can light the fireplace or candles or incense.

I can play music on a turntable or an MP3 player.

I can play live music on a guitar, piano, ukulele, or hang drum.

I can ring bells or make a prayer bowl sing.

I can walk back and forth in a room or walk a labyrinth
*   or walk in my neighborhood.*

I can do just about anything I want.

Got the picture? The smell? The sound? The feel? Maybe even the taste? Are you sensing the potential involvement of the whole body and soul in the experience?

THE GRID

Theoretically, a mental grid starts to develop if you list on one axis the *kinds* of prayer and on the other axis different creative *ways* you can pray. The result is incredible variety and almost endless possibilities. There is no longer any reason prayer should be synonymous with *boring*.

When you start to put it all together, a sample of one prayer experience could look something like this:

Praise — with singing a new melody to a Psalm of praise

Thank — through drawing symbols of things, people, events

Confess — by reading an ancient confession

Intercede — through doodling on friends' names and their needs

Contemplate — in lighting a candle and being still

Join — by lifting my hands toward the sky, expressing the desire to join God and his work on earth

All that's missing now is your own personal practice and experimentation. The following chapters will give you some solid ideas to try out and will allow you to create your own variations. I highly encourage you to experiment to find out what works for you, but also to leave your comfort zone, to be open to trying things you never thought you were good at or even associated with prayer before.

I know some things in the above list can be quite intimidating: improvisation, poetry, sketching, dancing . . . *yikes!* But as a trained composer, I said for years, "I do music, I don't do words," meaning I never felt competent enough to write text for my own music. Through expressing myself using words and text in my prayer times, I eventually surprised myself and entered into the world of poetry, which eventually led to my own published texts and even this book publication. *Voilà!*

Part
TWO

● ● ● ● ● ● ● ● ● ● ●

The following chapters will guide you through many possible prayer "courses." *I'll present my understanding of each course and its particular significance in the menu.*

Some of my personal experiences with each one will be included as well. At the end of each chapter, several practical recipes will be given that you can use right away or that may inspire your own inventions or variations.

So . . . now . . . put on your apron. Let's step into the kitchen together and see what's cooking.

Chapter 6

PRAISING

TELLING GOD HOW GREAT HE IS

In God you come up against something which is in every respect immeasurably superior to yourself. Unless you know God as that and, therefore, know yourself as nothing in comparison, you do not know God at all.
—C. S. LEWIS, *Mere Christianity*

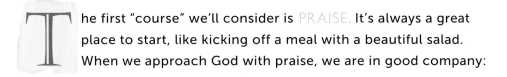

The first "course" we'll consider is PRAISE. It's always a great place to start, like kicking off a meal with a beautiful salad. When we approach God with praise, we are in good company:

- Isaiah started his spiritual experience, as recorded in Isaiah 6:3, with "Holy, holy, holy is the Lord Almighty; the whole earth is full of his glory."

- Many of King David's psalms as well as his final prayer open with classic lines of praise: "Praise be to you, LORD, the God of our father Israel, from everlasting to everlasting. Yours, LORD, is the greatness and the power and the glory and the majesty and the splendor, for everything in heaven and earth is yours" (1 Chronicles 29:10–11).
- Mary's heart explodes in praise with "My soul glorifies the Lord and my spirit rejoices in God my Savior" (Luke 1:46–47).
- Jesus begins his model prayer with "Our Father in heaven, hallowed be your name . . . " (Matthew 6:9).
- Paul launches into eloquent praise in the opening lines of his letter to the Ephesians: "Praise be to the God and Father of our Lord Jesus Christ, who has blessed us in the heavenly realms with every spiritual blessing in Christ" (1:3).
- The biblical list goes on: Melchizedek, Moses, Jethro, Ezra, Zachariah, Simeon, the shepherds, etc., etc., etc. They all knew what it was to enter into the presence of the Living God with the sweet taste of praise on their lips.

So let's briefly deal with some misconceptions about the word *praise*. Because of the rise of the "praise and worship" musical genre, there is a tendency among many to think that "praise" means singing a certain style of music, the words of which may obviously be about praising God, of course, but sometimes may also be egocentric and self-absorbed. "Should we start with praise?" in some circles would mean someone pulling out a guitar and everyone singing a few songs largely about asking God to do things to help them.

Uh . . . how do I say this? Praise is much, much bigger than this. With a quick look in a thesaurus, we can see that synonyms for the verb *to praise* include adore, appreciate, approve, celebrate, cherish, compliment, eulogize, honor, respect, revere, treasure, venerate, and worship. All of these verbs, grammatically speaking, require an object, and the object of any true praise is always the Eternal One.

In fact, there is a huge collection of words that languages employ in an attempt to capture our human sentiments of adoration, wonderment, and even stupefaction as we approach the beauty, magnificence, glory, splendor, wisdom of the Supreme Deity, the Creator, the Great One, the I AM. Many of these words are among the richest words that each language has to offer. They would be included on the Who's Who List of Superlatives. Yet, paradoxically, all remain incredibly inadequate in actually relating the intensity of this spiritual experience. Poets try to supersede language, reorganize words, and introduce new imagery. Musicians and artists attempt to avoid speech altogether. At times, works of art, architecture, literature, and music are indeed sublime; still all these noble attempts inevitably lack something as they try to portray the depths of a soul truly in awe of the One who was and is and ever shall be.

Space restraints here require me to distill this rich concept and its infinite variety of expressions down to just one word of six ink squiggles: *Praise*. I challenge you, though, to lavishly spend the rest of your lifetime exploring its vast, not-of-this-world dimensions. By its very nature, entering into praise can be elusive. I'm not sure we humanoids could handle a constant IV drip of transcendence even if it were an option, but I'd gladly volunteer to be the first to try!

Images that come to mind of my own diverse praise experiences range from a powerful Yellowstone geyser gushing up unexpectedly through my soul, to a shallow mud puddle where I am a small boy sitting in the middle recalling a visit to the ocean.

There are times when wonder and amazement dazzle us, when transcendence blazes uncontrollably around us, when we can't keep from saying a quiet "wow!" or lifting up an open hand toward heaven. There are other times when there is only a faint glow of glory in the

45

darkness or a strangely visceral sense that there is something beyond our five physical senses to be known, experienced, perhaps even tasted. With a little breath and patience, we can fan the smothered coals so that the spirit of adoration once again warms our souls.

One thing is certain: praise, adoration, worship (however you label the experience) is intended to be *all* about God. That means that it is *not* about us. I think for many, faith has been so focused on themselves for so long that they don't know how to let go of this self-obsessed orientation.

Occasionally I lead small groups in a Prayer Tasting, a sampler of the creative prayer practices described in this book. When it comes to expressing short phrases of praise, even though I give a clear definition of what praise is and what it is not, someone often speaks up to say how grateful they are for a blessing they've received. I'm thankful for blessings, too, but can't we take a few moments to shift the focus away from ourselves? I'm usually a nice guy and don't interrupt the group prayer, but I do always wish we could focus together exclusively on God's character and attributes for at least short periods of time.

In Richard Foster's exhaustive book on the subject of prayer, he states that "the Prayer of Adoration must be learned. It does not come automatically. Notice our children! They do not need to be trained to ask for things. The same is true for us. Thanksgiving, praise, adoration— those are seldom the first words in our minds . . . or on our lips. We need all the help we can get in order to move into a deeper, fuller adoring."[11]

The first and most important step in expanding, broadening, and deepening your personal experience with God is to learn to lead yourself in a few minutes of praise that focuses singularly and totally on God. Two words help to explain something about the importance and benefit of it:

1. Perspective. Praise radically changes our perspective. In actuality, God really doesn't need to hear from us about how great he is. He's known that for a long time. But you and I often *do* need to be reminded about how great he is since the day-to-day pettiness of our lives has a way of constantly dragging us down into the basement, and this is not where we want to live. Focusing on God's immensity, power, and magnificence changes the dynamic, the perspective, and pulls us upward, opens our horizons, gives us hope.

47

2. Portal. Praise is the portal to the presence of God. I often start out my prayer sessions telling God that I really don't feel like doing this again today, that I'm too tired, or I'm just not feeling spiritual. But with a little time devoted specifically to praise, I can and do eventually find a portal that opens up the closed door or clogged conduit deep inside my soul.

Enough of talking about it! Let's dive right into some practical ideas—some "recipes" for this important course.

LITANIES: I suppose my oldest idea for offering to God a few moments of personal praise (and the idea that has been the most effective for me personally) is this one. I "improv" my own litanies of praise with short phrases that highlight and list the names of God or the attributes of God, such as "God, you are _____." (Fill the blank with an adjective about God.) Or "Lord, your name is _____." (Fill in the blank with a name of God.) Say these aloud slowly, make complete sentences and morph them up a bit. Avoid the shortcut of only listing individual words. The idea here is to direct your words to God with deep respect, allowing the full phrases to bathe your soul until it feels softened. At some point, you may struggle to find more names/adjectives once you easily scrape off those on the surface of your mind. Keep pushing forward. There are almost always more, even better, deeper, and surprising ideas that come as you consider different aspects of God's character. With time, you can become poetic with these litanies, linking the ideas by similarity (the Light of the World, the Bright and Morning Star, the Sunrise on High) or by contrast (the Lion of Judah, the Lamb of God) or by alliteration (good, grand, great, graceful, glorious, generous) or . . . now it's your turn.

ALL OF CREATION: Read through Psalm 148 a couple of times. Do you see the big picture? Now take a full page of paper and draw symbols or pictures of the whole cast of creation (from angels in heaven to the sea monsters of the deep and everything in between) that this psalm illustrates. Make sure you draw a symbol of yourself too. Then read through the psalm again: "Let them praise the name of the LORD" (148:5). Explore other creative ways to focus on the psalms of praise.

THREE WORDS: Here's a little twist on another idea that helped me get into the praise mode. With paper and pen, I started with the letter "a" and wrote down three words that I associated with God: amazing, accepting, amicable, etc. Then I worked my way through the alphabet.

Because of the way my crazy brain works, I ended up switching between adjectives and verbs—I found the verbs meant more to me at the moment. I say this because I don't think you should let the structure of an exercise restrict your spirit. If you find a variation that works better, by all means "go with the flow." That said, you will find that you can potentially get bogged down in this prayer practice, that

God you are Free. God you are Wild

Lord your name is Holy

Lord your name is heavy on my tongue

it becomes a bit tedious, thinking of yet another word that starts with a certain letter. For me, it is helpful to persevere and push through these moments, to make my brain really work, to search deep into my soul for connections. Usually, I do find a simple yet significant nugget of inspiration that rewards my efforts.

For example, one morning I got to the letter *w* and to be honest, I was actually getting tired of the little game. I was feeling a sense of relief that it was almost over. Anyway, I searched for yet another word beginning with "w" when the word *weld* came to mind. *Strange,* I thought. *I've never thought of the word* weld *in relation to God or the spiritual world.* But there it was, a fresh new word and potential metaphor for my soul to play with, as seen in this journal entry.

Hmmm, what needs welding in my world? What has been welded together in my life? You know how when things have been welded together, there's that little scar? That seam? Everyone can see the imperfection but it doesn't really matter. For things to be welded, great heat is required, usually a blowtorch. It produces a flame so bright that it can only be viewed through a filtered glass. Makes me think of relationships that are bonded under the intense heat of difficulty, the camaraderie that is formed from liminal experiences,[12] or disorientating circumstances. My mind also thinks of those sculptures we've all seen of scrap steel junk welded together into some recognizable form. Could that be who I really am? That God's been able to make something of me by welding together the bits of "junk" in my life? I kind of like that idea!

(This reminds me of something I want to say before we get too deep in the list of ideas. There's no need to stress out over this or any other prayer practice. Be gracious and forgiving toward yourself when needed. Give yourself time to adapt to new ways to pray.)

TUMBLE, TUMBLE, TUMBLE: From my journal: *This morning I listened to my heart. She was full to the point of bursting with praise to God and wanting to express herself. (There are some overwhelmingly wonderful things going on right now in my life.) So as soon as I gave her a moment of calm (and with a cup of coffee in hand), my heart blurted out a soft whisper "I PRAISE You!" Followed by "I BLESS You!" Sensing the direction she was wanting to lead me, I, of course, followed. I asked my brain to help out.*

Do you have any similar verbs lying around that we might borrow? "I GLORIFY You! I EXALT You! I LOVE You! I TRUST You!" I slowly and thoughtfully repeated these simple phrases aloud totally randomly, allowing them to tumble around within me. Wanting to sustain the experience, I quickly consulted my handy little thesaurus and added to my litany: "I EXTOL You! I HONOR You! I REVERE You! I LAUD You! I ESTEEM You! I TREASURE You! I MAGNIFY You! I CHERISH You!"

Glancing at my list occasionally, I continued to allow the phrases to tumble randomly, tasting the nuanced flavor of each. Then the tumbling gently came to an end, I folded my hands together and my heart quietly said, "Thank You."

VERBAL REMIX: Another day I was searching for an opening course of praise when I came across Psalm 147. I read all the way through, looking for a recipe idea, something creative I could do with it, a different way of reading it maybe. *Wow, look at the verbs in this thing!* It's as if the writer of this psalm was actually concentrating on making a list of powerful verb phrases with a few phrases of praise mixed in to break the monotony.

Read through Psalm 147 for yourself. Write down the verbs and verb phrases (builds up, gathers, heals, binds up, counts, gives names, supports . . .). Read through the psalm again—aloud, this time—emphasizing with your voice each verb phrase.

Now give this psalm a remix by keeping the same form but changing the phrases and verbs to reflect divine actions you've seen in your own life adventure.

BODY PRAISE: What can you do with your body to communicate praise? Lifting your arms to heaven is the immediately obvious choice. Lay down prostrate and say nothing. Dance for joy. Jump up and down like a Maasai warrior. Create a movement that takes you from being closed in on yourself to slowly opening up to God. Enjoy!

ACCOMPANIED READING: I've had a lot of fun with this idea. I pick a psalm of praise or a great hymn of praise. Then I choose a piece of recorded instrumental music from my collection. It could be classical or ambient—I personally prefer something minimalist or even progressive jazz. Then I read out loud my text in sync with the music. It helps if the music is not too distracting and has some gaps in the texture allowing for good counterpoint between the text and the tune. Allow the rise and fall of the music to direct your reading of the text. This can have some surprising results! It can also fall flat. But that's OK—experimenting is fun.

MOVIE CHARACTERS: Think through some of the recent films you've seen and books you've read. Connect God's character to characters in movies, plays, and books that you admire or whose stories have touched you. Write these or say them aloud in a litany such as: God, you are even more giving than the young boy in the movie *Pay It Forward*. Lord, you are more gracious than Juliette Binoche's character in the film *Chocolat*. Father, you are far wiser and more powerful than Gandalf in *The Lord of the Rings*, and you bear the burden of our evil more than Frodo Baggins. Keep a running list.

53

SIMPLE SONG: If you have even a little musical ability, take a stab at making up a new melody for a particularly meaningful verse of praise. (Maybe the psalms actually mean it when they say, "Sing to the Lord a new song!") Or create a new version for an old hymn text—nothing like new music to give new meaning. Or just take the word *Alleluia* and improvise on it as a simple song. Don't work on perfection. It's just a simple gift, like a child's fistful of scraggly dandelions offered to a loving and appreciative Father.

WORD PLAY: Read through a psalm of praise, a classic prayer, or an old hymn and play with the key words. Here are some ideas: form a word cloud; make a crossword puzzle; create a Scrabble board; write key words randomly then doodle around them; write a haiku poem using them; form compound nouns from phrases (Lord, you are the "lifter of my head" = *head-lifter*—you may even invent new words if you need to); rewrite a portion of the text in your own free-verse or poetry format; or develop your own wordy ideas.

YOUR TURN: Invent your own "recipe."
- Grab a meaningful text that focuses on God—from an old hymnal, lectionary, a favorite quote, the Psalms, or write your own.
- Now do something with it—sing it, chant it, recite it, dance it, act it out, draw it, paint it, simplify it, graffiti it like a tag, print it out and doodle around on it, etc., etc., etc. . . .

Chapter 7

THANKING

REMINDING YOURSELF
WHAT GOD HAS DONE

If the only prayer you said was thank you, that would be enough.
—ATTRIBUTED TO MEISTER ECKHART

Piglet noticed that even though he had a Very Small Heart,
it could hold a rather large amount of Gratitude.
—A. A. MILNE, *Winnie-the-Pooh*

I f earlier we considered praise as a salad, then thanks is the soup. Psalm 100:4 encourages us to "enter his gates with thanksgiving and his courts with praise; give thanks to him and praise his name." Praise and thanks go so well together, like a delish' soup-and-salad lunch special. I find it helpful, though, to keep a bit of distance between them until each is understood fully and appreciated separately. While offering praise focuses exclusively on God and his attributes, giving thanks focuses essentially on what God has done. One is objective, the other subjective.

56

Giving thanks is perhaps the prayer most associated with the dining experience. For some, it may be the only prayer they ever say and perhaps only once a year when the extended family gathers together. Actually there are plenty of opportunities in a day to offer a brief prayer of thanks and plenty of reasons to do so.

Let's start with a little exercise: Try saying out loud the word *thanks*. It doesn't matter where you are. In just about any environment where you are reading this book, you should be able to say at least one word softly aloud without everyone around you thinking that you're crazy for talking to yourself. OK? So here we go . . . 3 . . . 2 . . . 1 —Thanks.

Now that wasn't all that bad, was it? Could we do it again and take it up a notch? This time, say aloud the words *thank you*. Ready . . . 3 . . . 2 . . . 1 —Thank you!

Stay with me, now. I'd like for you to think of someone in your life for whom you are thankful. Put the book down and ponder a few seconds the "why" behind your gratitude for this person: what they did, how they helped, how it made you feel, how they made a difference for you. Now with the thought of this single person still floating in your thoughts, say again the two simple words *thank you*. Do all you can to let these simple words carry the full weight of your appreciation for that person you are remembering.

Did you feel it? If you were paying close attention, it is possible that you experienced something ever so slightly: a subtle wrinkle in the spiritual fabric around you, a small ripple in the pond of your soul, a tiny glitch in the life matrix.

What exactly happens when we express gratitude for something? I'm not sure but *something* does happen! Here's another exercise, more like a homework assignment, that you probably can't do at this moment. We all sit down and have coffee or a meal one-on-one with a friend from time to time. You know how that goes, right? Too often it falls into the same rut of a little complaining about something, a little frustration with someone, some bragging about our latest possession, and maybe, on an inspired occasion, a little dreaming about the future. You've got the picture. Well, the next time one of these conversations with a good friend comes up, wait for the right moment and inject this thought: "Do you know what I appreciate about you?" Proceed to express your gratitude for their friendship, a positive characteristic of theirs, something specific they helped you with in the past, or even their simple willingness to spend time with you. Of course, be real and authentic about it—no need to go overboard or get syrupy.

Observe what happens next. How did it made them feel? Did it change the dynamic of the conversation? Sure, outwardly they may feel a bit embarrassed, awkward, or undeserving, but there's usually some sign that it has touched them deeply inside. I notice a certain look on people's faces when they are caught off guard in a good sense, and the look tells me (even though they don't say it), "Do you realize how rare it is to hear something that positive about myself?" or "Boy, you just don't know how badly I needed to hear something like that today!"

Now, think about how this expression of your gratitude to your friend made *you* feel. With just a few well-placed words, you've elevated the conversation. You've taken the relationship to a slightly higher plane. It's as if the café around you changed from fast food to elegant bistro. You've injected something good into the world that wasn't there before. If that makes you feel arrogant and self-congratulatory, then you're headed in the wrong direction. But when pure and simple gratitude carries you to a higher plane and if you

57

continue to live this way, expressing your gratitude for people and things more often, then you are entering a realm of life that is wider, deeper, and more firmly rooted in the spiritual.

If this type of thankful exercise with a friend has such positive consequences, the same can be true with God. Granted, he's *not at all* like our friends who may be starving for a little attention, but the process works very similarly on our part. When we take the time to express our thanks to someone else or to God, something happens—something happens in *us*! For one thing, it yanks us out of our default agendas of complaining, wanting, bragging, asking, etc. It changes the focus of the conversation, and it widens the lens angle to reveal a much bigger picture. It makes our heart just a bit softer, lightens the load we carry, and aims a spotlight on what really matters in life.

There are times in life when we really need what "thanks" has to offer us. Sometimes it is all we have to hold on to, like mom's homemade chicken soup when we're sick in bed with the flu. There's a little New Testament phrase that I grew up with that went something like "In everything give thanks . . . " (1 Thessalonians 5:17 ᴋᴊ21). On the surface it sounds nice and admirable, but it can be quite troubling when you try to drum up thanksgiving for things that are simply awful or unjust or cruel or devastating. There is just *no* way to be thankful for certain things that wreak havoc in our lives or the lives of others. As you may have observed, anyone who tries to be thankful by offering up fake Christian platitudes comes across as completely ridiculous.

I prefer to look at this verse from a different angle by remembering that no matter what I go through, even the worst tragedy of my life, I can find some things for which I'm thankful—maybe only one little thing, like fiercely focusing on the horizon when you find yourself on a small ship tossed about by the sea. At that moment, staring at that imaginary shoreline is all you have between you and full-blown seasickness.

So in the midst of meltdown, breakdown, burnout, washout or whatever, pause to reflect intently on specific moments from your past, even your distant past: that one friend who stuck by you, that one person who somehow helped you, that one thing a parent taught you, that one skill you know you have . . . then give thanks for that one thing.

59

This is an example of how "recipes" or "practices" often help guide my praying. There are times when I don't know what to do but I know what I've done before and I do it again. There are times when I need to give thanks without words. There are times when I don't think I can even begin expressing gratitude, but I can do a simple and seemingly insignificant activity and somehow, surprisingly, I'm carried to a different realm through a simple "game-like" practice.

When I set out to express thanks to God, I find it helpful to consider two different dimensions:

1. Creating time for intentional reflection and giving thanks for specific things, people, events, and developments.
2. Seeking ways to let my gratitude overflow and find expression in everyday life (for example, finding concrete ways to express my gratitude publicly). When reflection on gratitude teams up with demonstration of gratitude, they make an extraordinarily powerful combination.

Listed below are some sample ideas for injecting meaningful moments of thanksgiving into your prayer time.

60

PSALM REWRITE: I like to rewrite Psalm 136—you know the one with the phrase that repeats all the way through, "His love endures forever" (or something similar depending on your translation).

- Read it through one time in its original version.
- Go back and notice that at verse 9 the author begins to recount the story of the Exodus.
- Then, start at the beginning. Read it aloud slowly and thoughtfully. But this time at verse 9, substitute phrases of your own story (your own tale of exodus or suffering or even victory), taking your cue from the style of the Psalm, "to Him who_____"—each time repeating and even "tasting" the beautifully simple refrain, "His love endures forever." (I think saying it aloud is hugely important! The continual repetition serves as an aural reminder of the eternal and never-ending quality of God's love.)
- After you do that for as long as you like, jump back to the original ending of the Psalm at verse 23 to finish it off.

I think you'll agree it makes for a great start to a meal—a healthy mix of praise and thanksgiving.

variation 1: Here's something else to try next time you visit the beach: Sit in the sand where you can feel the waves wash around you repeatedly. You don't need a Bible. Recite phrases from your own story. Try to time the repetition of a phrase from your story and the phrase "His love endures forever" with each oncoming wave. Realize that you are in the presence of three classic symbols of "forever-ness": the sea, the sand, the sky. Soak it in. Let it cleanse you. Let it heal you. Feel the big picture. Feel God's presence.

SUPER SIMPLE POETRY: Simply list four things you're thankful for, followed by the word *thanks* or a phrase such as *I give you thanks* or even by the word *thanks* in other languages.

61

Loving wife : thanks
Healthy kids : thanks
Supportive parents : thanks
Diverse siblings : thanks

For my life — I give you thanks
For my home : I give you thanks
For my job : I give you thanks
For your calling : I give you thanks

Food : gracias
Friends : Merci
Family : obrigado
Fun : danke

SLICE OF LIFE:

Take just one "slice" of your life—focus on a moment of transition, of confusion, of illness, of inspiration, of transcendence. Then begin to "thank" your way through all the details: the people, the events, the decisions involved at that crucial time.

Feel free to express your gratitude however you feel at the moment: say it, sing it, draw it, write it, walk it, or eat it . . . the more variety, the better (and the more interesting).

variation 1: Give thanks silently for a slice of your amazing life the next time you are in the moment of eating a slice of amazing pizza . . . or pie . . . or cake . . . or . . .

variation 2: Use the "slice of life" perspective to practice many other kinds of praying. For example, take a slice of your life and pray a phrase of blessing or of intercession for the people who come to mind in that context.

BODY THANKS: How can you use body language to express your thanksgiving to God? Arms open wide in a position of receiving would be the first to come to mind. The book *Body Prayer* by Doug Pagitt and Kathryn Prill has many great examples. Here's one:

Body Prayer of Thanks

"Stand. Begin this posture from either your head or your feet. Touch your head, eyes, hands and feet (or do so in reverse order). When touching your head, eyes, hands or feet, curl your whole hand around that part of your body. Let the warmth or coolness merge from your hands to the body part; hold the touch as long as necessary to feel the interaction between skin touching skin, muscles acting against muscles, cells interacting to make up your body. If you traveled up your body as you prayed, now travel from the top down—or vice versa. Thank God for the gift of life and for the opportunities to participate in the continuing story of God. Lord, in this prayer, I thank you for my body.

"May I use all the abilities in my head to praise you,

May I see the lives through which you are active in this world,

May my hands further your story of creation,

May I walk in the ways you have established.

For this body, I pray."[13]

THE BIG LIST: Take out a big piece of paper. It could be your basic yellow legal pad or beautiful handmade paper. Start making a random list of people for whom you are thankful. I like to avoid the linear feel and instead write the names in all directions all over the page. The idea is to fill up the page and fill up your heart with thanksgiving. Name after name after name—even say "thanks" or "thank you" aloud with each name you write. Start with your childhood and work your way to the present. Don't let up until your page is full. Make an effort to recall even some seemingly insignificant people, the ones that you have almost forgotten and those who offered only a very simple kindness.

REMEMBER, RELEASE, REJOICE: This idea came to me while staring out an airplane window—one of those moments when, not only do I feel suspended in space, but time seems suspended as well.

Remember:

- Remember a relationship in your past, recall some of the special memories, and express gratitude for it.
- Think of a present friendship that you are thankful for and ponder the joy it brings you for a moment.
- Imagine a future friendship that you may have or hope to have and give thanks in advance for it.

Release:

- Recall a memory of a sad moment in your past and consciously begin to release the hurt associated with that memory.
- Think of something negative in your life right now and envision letting go of it.

- Consider a worry that you have about growing older and imagine it dissolving into thin air.

Rejoice:

- Remind yourself of something you are really proud of in your past and imagine a way to celebrate it properly.
- Recognize the importance of an activity that you are doing at this point in your life and be glad in the fact that you are mature enough to undertake it.
- Develop a plan for secretly helping/blessing someone in the near future and rejoice because of the joy it will bring to you.

THANKS BEFORE BED: This one was inspired by the book *Simple Abundance* by Sarah Ban Breathnach.[14] Just before going to bed, write down in a special notebook five things that you are thankful for from your day. Sarah stresses the importance of writing these down instead of simply thinking of them.

YOUR TURN: Dream up a new way to express your thanks: a personal hand sign or body movement to do even in public as a sign of your gratitude; a piggy bank or cookie jar or beautiful box of thanksgiving that you open only after you've totally filled it with scraps of paper "thanks"; create your own mantra or Gregorian chant of gratitude; make a collection of nature objects picked up in parks, on hikes, or in your own backyard representing various subjects of your gratitude. . . . Now it's your turn.

Chapter 8

CONFESSING

DEALING WITH LIFE'S REALITIES

Spirituality is not about being fixed;
it is about God's being present in the mess of our unfixedness.
—MIKE YACONELLI, *Messy Spirituality*

Or you might shout at the top of your lungs
or whisper into your sleeve,
"I hate you, God." That is a prayer too,
because it is real, it is truth,
and maybe it is the first sincere thought you've had in months.
—ANNE LAMOTT, *Help, Thanks, Wow*

kay, 'fess up: you really didn't want to read this chapter. I know, I know, it's because the words *confess, confession, confessionary* and every other member of this family . . . well, let's just say you don't look forward to these types coming over for dinner. (They do, however, have some very fun distant cousins: "confetti" and "confectionary" are a little more exciting to be around.)

This is a very emotional family, and not the happy, feel-good kind of emotions but the full-out drama kind. You've seen this family on hundreds of law-related TV shows, when nearly at the end, someone that we all least expect . . . *confesses*! Then suddenly there are gasps, tears, handcuffs, Miranda rights, squad cars—you know the routine.

For many, this family is also remembered for their somber, dark-walnut confessional booths and the old priest with bad breath who sits on the other side of the screen prescribing a few "Hail Marys" for the awful sin that took weeks to build up enough courage to confess.

Other confessions destroy families, end careers, lose elections. Let's face it—we've all been conditioned to just *not* enjoy being around this family at all.

However, there is an extremely high probability that if you are reading this book, then you are a human being. And as humanoids, we *all* have a strong propensity to make terrible decisions even when we realize at the moment they could sabotage our lives, careers, and the relationships we most cherish. Do I need to go into more detail or is your own list of past blunders already forming in your mind?

When we do these foolish things, that's when someone from the "Confession Clan" is likely to show up—like that one friend of yours who is not afraid to say right to your face the very thing you least want to hear. When a Confession family member starts whispering in your ear or hitting you with what seems to be a ton of bricks, you deplore the bane of their existence. Some time later, though, you will thank them for helping set things straight.

In other words, as human beings we will always find new and exciting ways to blow it as well as to revisit time after time our own particular classic screw-ups. Get used to it, because they will accompany you to the end of your days. If I could offer some advice here, I would say two things:

#1 Don't beat yourself up every time you "sin." God knows well our nature; he created us this way. He knows we will forever struggle with it. Learn to accept yourself as flawed—God certainly does. I have come to grips with the fact that in the morning I can have the loftiest of spiritual thoughts imaginable, but by the end of the day, I may have thoughts of utter disgust toward an annoying and smelly street person blocking the sidewalk. (If you need a home-work assignment here, do a study of major biblical characters and make a list of their faults. I think you'll find many of them were far worse sinners than you and me—i.e., Guys, you have surely wronged your wife in the past, but I doubt you've ever done to her what Abraham did to Sarah!)[15]

#2 Confess sin quickly. Get it over with and move on. These two points actually work together. The reason we don't want to confess immediately is because we haven't accepted our imperfection and we want to continue to believe that we have it within ourselves to be an almost perfect spiritual being. This causes us embarrassment when we come before God again and again. Get over it! Even when we are admittedly much less than we would hope to be, God immediately throws his arm around us and starts walking us forward again.

69

In my teen years, the word *confess* came to be inextricably associ-ated with *unconfessed sin*. Certain spiritual leaders at the time led me to believe that there was almost always hidden somewhere in the recesses of my memory some remaining unconfessed sin that was blocking the flow of God's victory in my life.

Then, as a young adult trying to rethink what prayer was, I found myself still in this default mode, still searching for the one lustful thought I had somehow forgotten in all my other times of confession.

Admittedly, there *are* spikes of serious sin that need to be dealt with immediately and appropriately. Unconfessed sin can be devastating to our spirit. However, most of us deal with the somewhat constant background noise of imperfection and personal disappointment that we experience living in the real and fallen world.

After a few years, thanks to some deeper, more insightful dialogue with the Confession Clan (who in my previous perception were all about keeping me feeling humiliated and worthless), they had a chance to recuperate their reputation. I'm pleased to say that we've now become good friends.

I think it started when I began noticing the confessions and creeds that we read together in church. Of course, many of them are older classics, but I remember discovering various modern versions of confessions that really resonated within me. Basically, confessions and creeds are well-crafted, formal statements of what we believe to be true about ourselves, our faith, and our God. One day, I had the out-of-the-blue idea of combining a classic creed with a not-so-well-crafted, informal statement of what I believed to be true about myself.

What I came up with was something that helped me instead of hurt me, that encouraged me instead of condemned me. It was as if I took a Polaroid of myself, wrote on that white space at the bottom "What you see is what you get," and then held it up to God. The wonderful thing that happened next was that God let me know that he understood, that things were still cool between us, and then gave me a big hug. Well, not really, but I think you know what I mean.

I must also "confess" that this change in my approach to confession was accompanied by a gradual shift in the way I saw my relationship with God. I think growing a bit older had a role to play as well. What I mean is that moral perfection, as much as I strove toward it, became less and less the ultimate goal of my faith. I realized that Jesus calls us to simply follow him, to flesh out his kingdom on earth, to become his hands and feet in this world. I think he realizes that we are inevitably going to do that as flawed (but continually being restored) individuals.

This leads to another important aspect of confession, and that is restoration. Confession's role is to lead us toward restoration. It's the part of this prayer that only God can do. We confess. God restores. We confess the reality of who we are, as damaged as we may be or as unholy as we may feel. God miraculously touches us somewhere deep within our soul and restores our relationship anew. Often this process reminds me of hearing theologian Jürgen Moltmann declare that, for him, the preeminent phrase in all of Scripture for understanding who God is would be "behold, I make all things new" (Revelation 21:5 KJ21). God keeps making things new, keeps renewing and restoring our relationship. Allow him to do it again.

Keep in mind that sometimes in between the confession and the restoration is a necessary action on our part—an action, such as releasing spiritually toxic habits or attitudes we've allowed to slip into our lives or perhaps offering an apology or retribution to someone we have wronged or offended. If you develop a practice of cultivating a spiritual environment that includes periodic confession, you can trust the Father to let you know when an action is needed and appropriate.

I hope you can begin to see confession as less of a threat and more as a friend—a friend that helps you get real with yourself and allows you to be who you really are. As you practice confession, make sure to build in the time and the sensitivity to welcome, experience, and embrace the restoration that naturally flows from confession. The following ideas may help you get going in the right direction.

71

WRITTEN CONFESSION: Write out a prayer of confession that is less based on your sins and more about the current reality of who you are . . . at this moment—such as this journal entry: *God, I confess to you that I'm a mere human being, I'm overly influenced by fear, hunger, sleep, pain, etc. . . . I'm sometimes fickle, indecisive, forgetful, arrogant, etc. . . . I can be compassionate and selfish in the same day, spiritual and materialistic in the same hour. The bottom line is: I need you.*

COFFEE CONFESSION: After each sip of your morning coffee, express aloud a statement about your present reality (feel free to be brutally honest with yourself): *I don't feel like doing this* . . . swig of coffee . . . *I'm still sleepy* . . . another sip of coffee . . . *I'm going to do it anyway* . . . coffee . . . *I think I may have some untapped potential* . . . coffee . . . *I like helping people* . . . coffee . . . *but I often disappoint myself* . . . coffee . . . . Continue until you've finished your cup. variation: A good hot tea works just as well.

CONFESSIO CORPO: Invent a body position, movement, or perhaps a dance move that signifies for you the act of confession and restoration. Often words get in the way and nonverbal communication needs to do the heavy lifting for us.

HYMN SING: There are some great classic hymns and simple, meaningful choruses that help us express our confession to God and renew our relationship with him. As you come across them in worship with your community, collect, keep, sing, and recite them.

CONFESSION COLLECTION: Similarly, you may also find that the well-written confessions of others, both ancient and modern, can be a rich treasure trove for your time of confession and restoration. Save and keep them with your other materials. When you feel inspired, try writing some of your own.

SYMBOL SEARCH: Keep on the lookout for symbols of confession and restoration in everyday life. As you see them, allow them to lead you through the process. For example, I see a simple potted plant as a powerful symbol—I am dirt. I am dirty. I am flawed and imperfect, yet something beautiful and life-giving comes forth from me—what is it? How does the miracle happen?

BREATHING: During a time of quiet stillness, allow your natural breathing to symbolize confession. As you exhale, think of one thing at a time that you wish to confess and release from your life. As you inhale, think of those things you long to breathe in and restore in your life. Exhale frustration—Inhale peace. Exhale doubt—Inhale assurance. Anger—Love. Selfishness—Giving . . . you've got the idea.

JOURNALING: A daily diary, a personal journal, the morning pages (from *The Artist's Way* by Julia Cameron[16]) or whatever you want to call them—the regular and ongoing process of recording your feelings, faults, anxieties, and ambitions—it is definitely a great way to stay real with yourself and to keep confession as a routine in your life. Invest in special notebooks. Make your own. Doodle. Collage. Collect. Cherish.

I AM: Once for a few brief moments of *reality check* (which is often my alternative way of saying *confession*), I pulled out my handy notebook and without thinking much about it, wrote the words, *I am . . .* then there was a long pause. I mention the pause because, probably like you, I rarely start these little practices feeling totally spiritual.

So, on the particular day mentioned above, I started with: *I am . . . here.* Then another *I am . . .* another long pause, but maybe not so long . . . *trying.* Yes, I am trying. Another *I am . . . still sleepy.* Yes, that's true as well, but maybe some coffee will help. *I am . . . blessed. I am . . . loved. I am cared for.* Yes, also true and for that I'm very thankful. *I am . . . less than perfect, I am . . . incomplete.* Yes, now we are getting into the real reality check. But despite that, *I am . . . useful . . . helpful . . . kind . . . making a difference . . . etc.*

It never ceases to amaze me how these simple, even trite ideas can be quickly transformative. Within a matter of minutes they can potentially take me from "I don't think this is going to happen today" to significant moments of reflection and even to that illusive spark of connectivity that lights up between my own inner spirit and the Spirit of my Creator. And for that, *I am . . .* truly thankful.

Chapter 9

BLESSING

SPRINKLING YOUR WORLD WITH GOODNESS

I will bless you . . . and you will be a blessing.
—GENESIS 12:2 (NIV)

A blessing is not a sentiment or a question;
it is a gracious invocation
where the human heart pleads with the divine heart.
—JOHN O'DONOHUE, *To Bless the Space Between Us*

fter living in Brazil for a few years and experiencing some very close friendships, I came to the conclusion that there were four things I would never be able to do as well as Brazilians, to the point of not even trying:

- Play *futebol* (soccer)
- Cook *churrasco* (barbecue)
- Dance *samba* (samba)
- Give a *despedida* (farewell blessing)

As wonderful as that list is, the last ability touched me the most. My Brazilian friends knew how to genuinely bless someone, and I didn't.

76

All it took was announcing an upcoming extended voyage, and I had the opportunity to experience personally one of the most beautiful things in the world—various friends and even neighbors (some I didn't think even knew me very well) would look me straight in the eye, place their hands on my shoulders, shake me just a bit to add effect, and then proceed to pronounce over me a long and fervent blessing. And they weren't even all "religious" people!

Their pronouncements typically went something like this:

May your journey be safe,
May your time away be blessed,
May your family experience good health,
May you enjoy delicious food,
May you be filled with happiness.

At this point, if the friend who doing the blessing was "on a roll," it could easily spin off into a blessing for the whole rest of my life.

May your days be long and full,
May your life be peaceful,
May your children be successful,
May your children give you many grandchildren,
May you . . .

Then, they would realize that I was just going away for a few months and they would bring it back to a close.

And may you have a safe and pleasant return back home to our neighborhood.

Lastly, there was always one final strong shake of the shoulders followed by a huge and enthusiastic hug.

Linguistically, these pronouncements were a parade of subjunctive verbs. If you speak a Latin-based language, you'll know that the subjunctive mood sounds so much more eloquent and poetic than our milder English equivalent.

Whenever I had the privilege of being on the receiving end of one of these super-blessings, I simply stood there motionless in total receptivity, downloading and installing it all, as if upgrading my entire emotional operating system. I wanted all of everything they had to give me. But during a typical "shower of blessing," I invariably had a few different thoughts going through my head:

- I don't know how to do this at all in return! I'm totally "blessing-challenged." But hey, where I grew up, my family and friends didn't do this. It just didn't happen. My dad never held my shoulders and blessed me. My mom didn't either. Not even a close friend and certainly never a neighbor.
- There is something very significant and humbling about simply receiving and not having anything comparably eloquent to say in return—only a measly inadequate "obrigado" (thank you) at the end.
- Although I had nothing to offer in return, I came to understand that there was something beneficially reciprocal happening to the people who were blessing me. For a few minutes, they suspended their normal egocentric lives, placed a fellow human in higher priority than themselves, and expressed their hopes for the other's peace and well-being. In so doing, they inevitably lived life on a higher plane, if only for a few moments. It always smelled like the kingdom of God to me.

Fast-forward a decade or so and I started reading books on Celtic spirituality. *The Celtic Way of Evangelism*[17] and *How the Irish Saved Civilization*[18] were often pulled out of my bag on the Montréal metro during my irregular commutes around the city. I also bought other books that simply contained ancient Celtic prayers and blessings. These touched me so deeply that I wrote music to several of them. They were *terre à terre,* earthy texts, amazingly fresh to me, despite being centuries old.

In 2006, I went to the Greenbelt Festival in England for the first time. Greenbelt is a wonderful three-day event where over 20,000 people gather to focus on three of my favorite topics: art, faith, and justice. After reading the short description about the various events and speakers, Sanan and I along with daughter Jacki decided to check out a guy called John O'Donohue, glibly saying, "So . . . if he's not interesting we'll jump to something else." The Irish poet/theologian started out his talk by reciting one of his blessings entitled *"Beannacht"* (a Gaelic word for blessing). As he continued his talk, it became one of those moments when we just looked at each other with raised eyebrows, silently trying to communicate that what we were listening to was truly special. Little did we know that this extremely gifted and deeply spiritual poet-mystic (who was my age, by the way) would leave this world only a few short months later.

In the years to follow, after moving to Paris, I listened over and over to the podcast of that talk and especially to O'Donohue's opening blessing. I was so touched by it that I pondered it, analyzed it, and began to write my own version of blessings, borrowing from his poetic structure. While waiting on friends at the airport or for someone to stop by and enjoy the art in the gallery where I worked, I began to develop a taste (and later a full-blown appetite) for crafting well-thought-out blessings.

Blessings have been a rather recent entry into my gourmet menu of prayer possibilities. Perhaps they are like something as refined as truffles or lobster—not necessarily for everyday but quite a wonderful way to occasionally treat yourself and others.

So, how do we get started with blessing people? I think the best way is to hear from John O'Donohue himself. Here's a little motivation from the introduction of his book *To Bless the Space Between Us: A Book of Blessings*:

> *In the parched deserts of postmodernity, a blessing can be like the discovery of a fresh well. It would be lovely if we could rediscover our power to bless one another. I believe each of us can bless. When a blessing is invoked, it changes the atmosphere. Some of the plenitude flows into our hearts from the invisible neighborhood of lovingkindness. In the light and reverence of blessing, a person or situation becomes illuminated in a completely new way. In a dead wall a new window opens, in dense darkness a path starts to glimmer, and into a broken heart healing falls like morning dew. It is ironic that so often we continue to live like paupers though our inheritance of the spirit is so vast. The quiet eternal that dwells in our souls is silent and subtle; in the activity of blessing it emerges to embrace and nurture us. Let us begin to learn how to bless one another. Whenever you give a blessing, a blessing returns to enfold you.*[19]

And here are some "how to's" for various genres of blessings (as you practice them, may many blessings return to "enfold you" as well):

BENEDICTUS: Think of a friend—visualize him or her—and now pronounce aloud the Latin word *benedictus* (or you could say "blessing" or "bless them" or "may they be blessed"). Consider the network of friendships that you share with that person. From that network choose another friend—visualize that person—and pronounce your blessing on him or her. Allow a crazy, random, free association of friends to parade through your mind as you sprinkle blessings on each.

SETTING FOCUS: Take some time to focus on just one person you want to bless. Imagine him or her placed in various beautiful settings that represent a place of well-being and joy. For instance:

- Standing in a tropical waterfall, with eyes closed and arms extended as if receiving all the waterfall has to offer
- Standing on a mountain top as a single ray of sunlight bursts through the heavy clouds and shines right on them
- Seated on the sand of a calm beach with wave after gentle wave washing up around them

Variation 1: Draw a picture of your friend(s) in one of these settings.

Variation 2: Take a few minutes to send a letter or e-mail of encouragement or appreciation. (Include the picture if you want.)

CRAFT A BLESSING: Try your hand at writing out a blessing for someone. The form is a bit unique. It is poetic in the sense that it is rich in metaphor and imagery but without necessarily following the prescribed rhythm of poetry. Many or all of the lines could begin with "May . . . " or you may want to employ a couplet idea of "When . . . so-and-so happens—May . . . this happen." Allow yourself time to craft a beautiful work of art. It could take days. A blessing can be for a certain person or for a specific occasion. Or it can be generic in the sense that it applies to the general human condition each of us confronts and deals with in life.

CLASSIC BLESSINGS: As you envision a friend you want to bless, stretch out your hand as you may have seen your pastor or priest do at the end of a service. Read one of the classic biblical blessings: Numbers 6:24–26, Romans 15:13, 2 Corinthians 13:13 or 14, Galatians 6:18, 1 Thessalonians 5:23, 2 Thessalonians 3:16, Hebrew 13:20, or adapt a blessing from the Book of Common Prayer or some other at-hand liturgical sources. Feel free to adapt and expand on any classical blessing.

SCRABBLE YOUR BLESSING: On a blank piece of paper, start with a word like *bless, blessing, benedictus,* or even better a friend's name. Play freestyle Scrabble as you attach additional words of good and positive things you wish to include in your blessing for this person.

82

ENCIRCLE: Imagine that the person you want to bless is standing in the middle of the room with eyes closed and hands out to receive your blessing. Walk or even dance around as you visualize encircling them with words of encouragement and blessing.

BIG FAT BLESSING: I like to write out a friend's name in large, fat letters. In the space within the letters, I draw symbols or write words and phrases of blessing that I want to include. This is fun to do in multiple colors with pencils, pens, or paints. If you do a particularly nice job, consider giving it to your friend.

IRISH BLESSINGS: You've probably seen this classic Irish blessing on a plaque in someone's home:

May the road rise to meet you,
May the wind be always at your back,
May the sun shine warm upon your face,
The rains fall soft upon your fields and,
Until we meet again,
May God hold you in the palm of His hand.

There are many more Irish blessings out there if you do a quick Internet search. Collect them and use them as you weave the practice of blessing into your prayers. You'll notice that Irish blessings are very simple and practical, usually inspired by elements of nature. Allow them to inspire you to write your own.

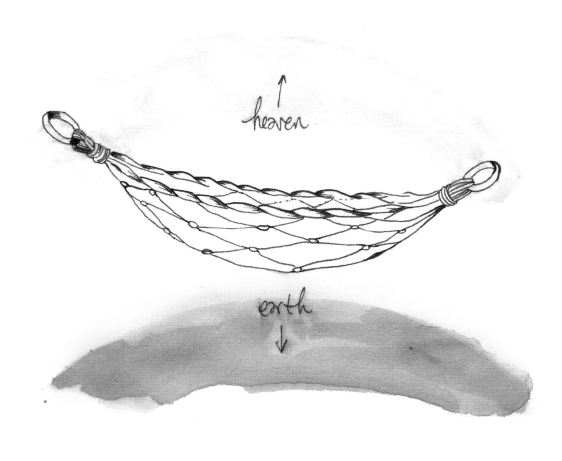

Chapter 10

OBSERVING

RECOGNIZING GOD'S PRESENCE AROUND YOU

*I think it pisses God off if you walk by the color purple
in a field somewhere and don't notice it.*
—ALICE WALKER, *The Color Purple*

*Look for God. Look for God like a man with his head on fire
looks for water.*

—ELIZABETH GILBERT, *Eat, Pray, Love*

I n Rio, my sacred space was in a hammock on the veranda, suspended between heaven and earth. At that time, reaching high above me was a huge avocado tree. It came quite naturally as I was experimenting with new possibilities in prayer to include the avocado tree in the process. After all, this magnificent tree was a perpetual and faithful witness to all that had been and was transpiring there.

One day, after a little taste of praise and thanksgiving appetizers, I pulled out a yellow legal pad and began writing down my thoughts about the tree. The list started out slowly but eventually included:

- Its branches are like arms lifted up in praise.
- Its leaves are open to receive the gracious gift of sunlight.
- It is deeply rooted.
- It has a river of life flowing in its veins in the form of sap.
- It shows signs of suffering—broken branches, diseased leaves, insect attacks.
- It helps others by providing shade or by offering a safe place to live above the dangers on the ground.
- It may have a legacy—on a grand scale, its wood could be used for furniture or a house that could be passed on to generations. In a simpler way, it could provide fertilizer for new growth after its death.
- It bears fruit, which it freely gives as nourishment and pleasure for others (and lots of guacamole for me).

I proceeded to completely fill a whole legal page with my observations.

A few months later, while on a youth retreat in a remote setting in Brazil, I was informed just before bedtime that I was scheduled to lead the devotional the following morning. Now, unless you've lived and worked in another language, you may not fully appreciate the surge of anxiety that occurs at a moment like this—even worse, just before bedtime. Improvising a devotional talk first thing in the morning for fifty people in a language that you're still learning—well, I think the word *panic* describes the situation rather well.

Maybe it was my desperate panic-prayer that somehow reminded me of the laid back, peaceful times under the avocado tree, but the brilliant idea of leading the entire group in a similar experience came to my mind. Early the next morning I went outside, cut a large branch off a tree and dragged it into the meeting spot. After standing it up as if it were actually a tree (at least I had everyone's attention), I asked the group to observe this "tree" for a few minutes and to make a list together of the common characteristics we all share with it. After the initial expressions of bewilderment and deafening silence, the first few ideas began to surface. The group went on to create their own full-blown and meaningful devotional time simply by observing a gift of nature.

I love the way Richard Foster describes how to start with this kind of praying in his book *Prayer: Finding the Heart's True Home*:

We learn about the goodness of God not by contemplating the goodness of God but by watching a butterfly. So here is my counsel: begin by paying attention to the little creatures that creep on the earth. Do not try to study or analyze them. Just watch the birds and the squirrels and the ducks. Watch, do not evaluate, watch.

Go to a brook and splash some water onto your burning face. In that instant do not seek to solve all the problems of pollution and the ecosystem; just feel the water. Most of all do not try to find God in the water or to make yourself thankful for the water. Simply allow the cool wetness to refresh your skin. Now sit back and listen to the sound of the brook. Watch the branches of the tree overhead swaying back and forth. Notice the leaves fluttering in the breeze—notice their shape, their color, their texture. Listen to the symphony of the rustling

88

leaves and the scampering chipmunks and the twittering birds. Remember, I am asking you not to analyze, only to notice.

When we do these kinds of things with some degree of regularity, we, in time, begin to experience pleasures rather than merely scrutinize them. What this does within us is altogether wonderful. We are first drawn into these tiny pleasures and then beyond them to the Giver of pleasures. True pleasures are, after all, "shafts of the glory," to use the phrase of C. S. Lewis. As this happens, thanksgiving and praise and adoration will flow naturally in their proper time: "To experience the tiny theophany is itself to adore."[20]

Decades later and living in Europe, while observing nature is still a rich source of spiritual inspiration, I now see God around me in my urban context as well. Along with my Dutch friend, Willemijn de Groot, we lead retreats which we call the Cache-Cache Expérience.[21] (*Cache-cache* is French for *hide and seek*.) We invite people to join us for a couple of days in Paris or Amsterdam to search together for meaning, metaphor, inspiration, insight, and maybe even a touch of transcendence in the noisy, crowded, busy context of these European cities. We encourage participants to capture or document their experience using their particular creative gifting: photography, video, journaling, poetry, music, songwriting, drawing, painting, dancing, etc.

I love the way Willemijn, at the beginning of each Cache-Cache Expérience, makes this statement: "Jesus lived in a rural context. When he walked through wheat fields, he stuck out his hand, grabbed some wheat and used it as a metaphor, 'Unless a kernel of wheat falls to the ground and dies, it remains only a single seed . . . ' (John 12:24). For those of us who live in an urban context, if we stick out our hands or look around us, what will we find? What might we learn? What inspiring metaphors will appear?"

I encourage you to occasionally include this simple idea of observation in your prayer diet. It especially works well if you're outside in a park, in a forest, on vacation, or simply looking out your window. Beware that it takes some time and some practice, plus being very attentive, to begin seeing God "hiding" in the world around you. (Be comforted, though, knowing that God often acts like a kind grandfather playing hide-and-seek with children—coughing loudly or bumping the furniture on purpose, actually wanting to be found.)

Here are a few ideas to help you add observation to your prayer menu. Be ready for some interesting and inspiring moments.

GO-TO CLASSIC: What works best for me is what I did that day under the avocado tree—pull out a paper and start jotting down thoughts, observations, and insights. It is important to remember that this takes some mental and spiritual energy. If you're like me, there is always a little voice that pipes up early in the process with something like: *Hey, I thought we were here just to chill out and relax?* If you push through the temptation to just do nothing, continue to encourage yourself to reflect, take time to carefully observe what is around you, then begin to think metaphorically and even poetically, you *will* be rewarded.

variation: Do the same exercise with symbols or pictures.

TWELVE-MONTH CYCLE: Decide upon a list of twelve common elements found in nature. Choose one per month over the course of a year to focus on and use as a theme for prayer, reflection, poetry, art projects, etc. Examples: Rock, Sky, Water, Snow, Rain, Tree, Flower, Sun, Moon, Stars, Mountain, Dirt, Grass.
variation: Use a quarterly or seasonal cycle.

ARTISTIC CAPTURE: Observation is a form of prayer where the arts can come to your aid and play a powerful role. As you observe and contemplate beauty in nature, people, or circumstances, respond by capturing the moment through drawing, sketching, painting, dancing, photographing, filming, composing, or even waxing poetic.

RAIN: We usually consider rain a downer. Sure, it makes everyday life a bit more complicated, but we can also see it as an aspect of nature that shows up randomly and gives us another chance to seek inspiration. Here are some ideas:

- Watch rain as it hits your window. Raise the window a bit and listen to it, smell it, and feel it. What comes to your mind?
- I know this sounds crazy, but consider taking a walk in the summer rain without a raincoat or umbrella (or even shoes). Feel the rain soak through your clothes, run down your face. Let it remind you of your baptism. Allow it to symbolically wash you clean. Lift your arms toward heaven in thanksgiving for this life-giving gift. If you're really feeling crazy, run, sing, shout, and even dance around a bit. (Best done in an isolated context, far from your curious neighbors.)

- Find a place where the rain makes an interesting noise or music, even a melodic gurgle. Take advantage of it as a beautiful and natural accompaniment to your prayer.

91

PEOPLE IN THE PARK: I enjoy watching people in parks. Often, all stages of life are represented. You may see parents who love their children, business people seeking a few moments of calm, men playing chess, children conquering the jungle gym, older people escaping the boredom of small flats, lonely people, happy people, tired people, sad people. Many of them are being refreshed by having time to relax and breathe some fresh air. Take time yourself to relax, breathe, and be refreshed in a public park. Allow the constant parade of humanity to speak to you. Allow God to speak to you through them.

SEASONAL FAVORITES: Throughout the year, choose four favorite spots in your environment—one for each season of the year. Be attuned to the lessons and blessings of each season as you sit, spend time, observe, reflect, and pray. For example, choose a beautiful winter scene after a snowfall or a simple forest of bare winter trees. Springtime could be spent in a garden full of flowers or beside a bubbling mountain brook. Summer may be enjoyed anywhere, either on a warm sunny day or a lazy summer evening while listening to crickets. Fall could be under your favorite tree as it drops its colorful leaves. Turn each of these chosen spots into special sacred spaces for seasonal prayer retreats. Allow each place to "do their thing" on you year after year.

MUSEUM MEDITATION: Once I lived in a town that had a small but excellent free museum. I went there often, especially when I was nearby with some time to kill. Besides great paintings, there were beautiful handmade rugs on the floor and lovely leather chairs to sit in, not to mention the inspiring modern architecture by Frank Lloyd Wright. Try out a museum sometime, perhaps one near your home or where you vacation. Avoid the temptation to see all the museum has to offer and instead, spend twenty minutes in front of a Rembrandt or in a room full of Greek sculptures or slowly walking through a gallery of modern art. Engage your spirit with beauty and see what it does for you.

FOREST WALK: Autumn is a great time of the year to take a long walk in the woods. Even beyond the gorgeous changing colors of the leaves, a forest is full of symbolism and metaphors for all of life. However, these take some time to discover . . . and can only really be appreciated by experiencing them.

So here's your assignment: Get yourself out of the city or suburbs and go to a nearby forest. Take a long walk on a well-marked trail. If you are alone, feel free to talk out loud to the forest friends (trees, vines, leaves, bugs, squirrels, dirt, etc.) you meet along the way. Call them by name and tell them what you find especially beautiful about them and why they are meaningful to you.

If you are not alone, discuss with your friend that you'd like to search for meaning, beauty, and metaphorical wisdom in the forest and dialogue about it. One idea is to walk in silence to a certain destination and then discuss your observations on the return trip. If you need more help, here's a list of way-too-many suggestions that we sometimes use with Cache-Cache groups. Choose just two or three that seem meaningful and appropriate in your setting.

- Look for something that reminds you of mystery.

- What disturbs you? Think about why.

- Touch something that is a metaphor for the greatness of God.

- Write a parable based on something you observe.

- What are you afraid of? Think about what that tells you about yourself.

- Find something that reminds you of the imminence (closeness) of God.

- Look for something that is a metaphor of what you want to do with your life.

- Make a list of adjectives that describe what you see.

- Look for something that reminds you of the incarnation.

- If something around you could talk, what would it say to you? Write down its message.

- Smell the air—what does it tell you?

- Find something that represents your idea of following the way of Jesus.

- Where do you see love expressed?

- Look for something that reminds you of the kingdom of God.

- Take a deep breath, realizing it's a breath of life. Take another one. And another one. . . .

- How do you sense God's presence here?

- Count the colors around you.

- What examples of resurrection do you see?

- Describe the contrasts you notice around you.

- What would you like to change? Think about how.

- Write a haiku poem about what you see around you.
  (3 lines: 5 syllables, 7 syllables, and 5 syllables)

- Is there something you see that makes you hopeful?

- Pick up something and hold it . . . until it "talks" to you.

- Touch something that touches you (my personal favorite).

Chapter 11

LAMENTING

ALLOWING SADNESS
FOR THINGS UNFIXABLE

There is a time for everything . . .
a time to weep and a time to laugh . . .
—ECCLESIASTES 3:1, 4

The darker the night, the brighter the stars,
The deeper the grief, the closer is God!
—FYODOR DOSTOYEVSKY, *Crime and Punishment*

There are times in life when you need to allow yourself to be sad, when it is appropriate to lament, when your soul cries out to mourn. It could be after the senseless slaughter of innocent school children by a crazed gunman or on becoming aware of the systemic evil of human trafficking on a global scale or upon learning of the untimely death of someone you love. Let me suggest that instead of fighting this natural urge, you not only allow it to happen but encourage it. Not only encourage it, but decide to do it well—intentionally create a special time and space to lament.

It may seem weird, but there's something about lament that I welcome. Tragedy has a cruel way of ripping off the masks of self-sufficiency and self-satisfaction. It yells in the streets, "No! Everything is not A-okay!" It cracks apart our airtight theologies about God having everything under control. It forces us to get real and really struggle with the big questions of life. It cautions us that this life journey we are on is not easily comprehended with a few sermon points but demands a lifetime of wisdom to even begin to fathom. Allowing yourself space to intentionally lament signifies that you are beginning to adjust to and accept the untidiness of real-life spirituality.

Keep in mind, though, that lamentation needs to be sandwiched together with other kinds of prayer. Just as a feeble-legged friend walks best when being propped up on both sides by understanding and cooperative friends, Lament is healthier when Praise and Thanksgiving come alongside to lighten the load. The practice of lamenting will take some time and some thought. It may seem strange at first. But eventually your soul will thank you. Here are some practical suggestions:

LAMENT ART: Let your personal giftedness lead the way. How does your unique soul prefer to express itself? Does it write words or draw pictures? Does it sing songs or dance to rhythms? Does it take pictures or video? Does it prefer poetry or prose? Oils or collage? Piano or guitar? You don't have to be a professional. This may even be your first foray into the arts. No one ever has to see it or hear it, but set aside some time for your soul to express its sadness through art. There is a depth of your soul that runs much deeper than words or platitudes. This is precisely where art and metaphor are your soul's best friends. Begin working on a project that addresses a sadness in your human spirit. Let the artistic expression be just for you. Don't get sidetracked by thinking of other people's opinions or even your own deep feelings of grief or insecurity. This art will be between you and God. Know that he understands the feeling behind every brush stroke, each phrase of song or each layer of clay.

CONTROLLED LAMENT: I set aside time occasionally for what I call a "controlled lament" and find it spiritually therapeutic. It is not a time to "fix" the situation, nor even a prayer for God to fix it. Rather, it is a time when I share just a fraction of a glimpse of the extreme anguish of God's own heart. Here is an example of how a tragic shooting might be lamented. First of all, I select some appropriately mournful music. My usual choices are Henryk Górecki's Symphony No. 3, "Sorrowful Songs" and Samuel Barber's Adagio for Strings, op. 11.

You may also want to select an object or image that you can hold in your hand to help you focus on the particular tragedy (perhaps a photograph, a certain color, flower, toy, clothing, or jewelry—anything that could represent some aspect of the sorrow you feel). A pencil and paper will allow you to journal your thoughts. Now, with the music playing and the object or image in hand, simply allow yourself to be sad. You may cry.

I find it helpful to divide the tragedy up into imaginary rooms that I can slowly enter and empathize with the people who are there. First, I think about the victims themselves . . . the dreams that may have been lost . . . the lives that were cut short . . . the fear and pain they may have endured. Second, I let my mind think about the overwhelming sorrow of the family and friends, as if to share in it with them, to help them carry it, if only for a few moments. Next, I reflect on the community that will never be the same—that name, when mentioned, will forever carry a tragic connotation. I then move to the room of the perpetrator(s) . . . their family and friends . . . their confusion. I offer a prayer of thanksgiving and encouragement for the professionals who may have suffered their own hidden scars from holding at bay their emotions while dealing with mutilated bodies, bloodstained walls, and distraught family members. Then I leave time for silence. Again, there is communication that happens on the soul level that is far deeper than rational thoughts and words.

Finish the time of lament with a prayer for yourself . . . that you may continue to have faith in God and even in humanity despite this shocking evidence to the contrary . . . that you may continue to be a force for good in the world, to inject grace, to show acceptance, to practice random acts of kindness, even if in very small ways. Then offer a prayer of thanksgiving for those who are dear to you. You may want to read a comforting or encouraging prayer or Scripture passage aloud to conclude.

LAMENT LETTERS: For many, writing is the best way to deal with an aching heart. May I suggest that you write down your feelings in the form of letters (or journal entries) addressed to the various people involved in the tragedy at hand? Let them know you hurt with them. If you're dealing with a large-scale situation, you could invent a fictitious person that represents a larger group. (For example, write to a fifteen-year-old named Marie to represent the teenage girls being trafficked in the sex industry.) You may even want to write a scathing letter directly to God himself to vent your anger and frustration. He *can* handle it, by the way.

LAMENT VENT: Others may need to have a trusted friend around to help deal with serious lament, one they don't mind shedding a few tears with. Being this kind of friend really helps those grieving the loss of a family member. In order to raise the level of the exchange from normal conversation or uncontrolled grief to something of meaningful significance, consider creating a simple spiritual meal:

> Read a short portion of praise from the Psalms and then spend a good amount of time being thankful for good times and precious memories. Jot down notes if you want to preserve the memories that are recalled. Now allow time to lament, to express the inexpressible pain, the loss, the separation, the solitude, the instability that you feel. Remember that tears are a part of lament; it's more than okay to let them flow freely. Conclude with a prayer for yourself and the entire family. Have a few family photos handy so you can look at each individual and pray for them by name.

Unfortunately, there will be too many opportunities to practice this prayer. Sometimes it is incited by random events, sometimes by ongoing evil and systemic injustice in the world. Know that when needed, creative lamentation can express something far beyond words and begin to bring its unique comfort to a sorrowful soul.

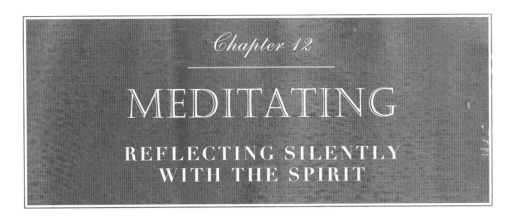

Chapter 12

MEDITATING

REFLECTING SILENTLY
WITH THE SPIRIT

*The best contemplative tradition is often inclined
to pass on from listening to a tranquil beholding.*
—HANS URS VON BALTHASAR, *Prayer*

I f you don't mind, I'd like to consider the next two types of prayer together just a bit. They are often misunderstood, confused, and frequently used synonymously.

It has taken me quite a while to understand the subtle differences between meditation and contemplation. It's like studying a pair of twins until you realize that there *are* slight differences in their noses and then you, of course, feel embarrassed for staring at them too much. I admit to having been slow to understand the more subtle differences in these spiritual practices, but I must also throw in my excuse—very few people along my journey have helped me with this. For most of us, there has been a lack of comprehensive instruction offered when it comes to differing kinds and methods of praying—the very *raison d'être* of this book.

Back to our not-so-identical twins, meditation and contemplation—the difference between them is actually quite simple. They are both introspective, quiet, and reflective, but Meditation is stimulated by something external: a text, a quote, a sound, an image, a thought, or even a repetitive action, while contemplation deals with the purely internal: silence, stillness, void, release, and the lack of emphasis on reasoning and rational thought.

For many Christians through the centuries, these two practices have worked in tandem, a lot like two pedals on a bicycle:[22] meditation on a text leading quite naturally to contemplation involving moments of silent reflection or "beholding" as Hans Urs von Balthasar and Madame Guyon call it.

Still, I realize that discussing these two can get tricky because some spiritual traditions use the term *meditation* to refer to what the classic Christian world calls *contemplation*. Confused? Stay with me. Perhaps it will help to "do something"—something more *practical* than theoretical. Try this out sometime: After you have begun praying with praise, thanksgiving, and confession, open your Bible to a few verses that have already been meaningful to you. (Remember, though, this is not Bible study time.) Simply read them, perhaps several times. After each reading, pause to reflect on phrases, to taste them, chew on them. In this way you are "meditating" on these words. You are, in fact, following in the rich tradition of David as seen throughout the Psalms (i.e., Psalm 119:15, 23, 27, 48, 78, 97, 148).

If you take it one step further and sit in silence for just a few minutes—not really processing or thinking about the text, but just remaining open to receive whatever God wants to give you—then you have moved into contemplation.

Once the silence seems to have run its course, you may look back at the text or image that has inspired you, intentionally thinking about it and meditating on it again, this time from a different or deeper perspective. Then move back into the silence and stillness of contemplation. Cycle back and forth as long as your spirit feels there is something there.

Some of my Protestant and evangelical friends have a problem with the word *meditation* because it is so widely used in other religions and the New Age movement. I'd like to push back a bit on this reaction with three thoughts:

1 Meditation is a thoroughly biblical practice. A quick word search will reveal a wide variety of passages in Genesis, Joshua, Psalms, and a couple in the New Testament, even in the King James Version.

2 Meditation is a spiritual human activity like mourning, fasting, or praying and is not limited only to one religious group while remaining unavailable to others.

3 Meditation and contemplation are in some ways more mature means of praying. Practicing them signals that you have moved beyond default-mode praying—simply asking for things for yourself or for others around you. It indicates that your relationship with God is changing from a monologue to a dialogue.

I love the way Charles Spurgeon puts it in his sermon on meditation:

> *Our bodies are not supported by merely taking food into the mouth, but the process which really supplies the muscle, and the nerve, and the sinew, and the bone, is the process of digestion. It is by digestion that the outward food becomes assimilated with the inner life. Our souls are not nourished merely by listening awhile to this, and then to that, and then to the other part of divine truth. Hearing, reading, marking, and learning, all require inwardly digesting to complete their usefulness, and the inward digesting of the truth lies for the most part in meditating upon it.*[23]

Give meditation and contemplation a try—perhaps they will take some getting used to, but once you do get accustomed to them, you'll find they are like *filet mignon* or *filet de sole*—the very heart of a gourmet meal.

Being silent but relaxed and attentive to the Divine Presence bonds our relationship like nothing else. Here are some ideas that could help you go a bit deeper:

- Find a short passage in the Bible that has already touched you in the past.

- Read through it slowly aloud, then pause for a minute. Think about the structure, grammar, context, intent, or whatever helps you begin to understand what the text is communicating.

- Read through the passage again aloud; pause for about two minutes. During this pause, consider which phrase is the most interesting to you. Taste it. Chew it. Try to memorize it by re-reading it a few times. What are these verses encouraging you to do? Who are they inspiring you to be? Can you use these phrases to intercede for others or yourself?

- Read through the text one last time, again slowly and out loud. Take about a three-minute pause. But this time try *not* to think or analyze or process the verses . . . just be quiet and listen . . . receive, enjoy, behold . . . simply savor the moment. If your mind wanders into thinking about the stuff you need to get done today or something you forgot to do yesterday (which is completely natural), just note it down to be dealt with later and repeat again the meaningful phrase you just memorized.

If you've managed to accomplish this relatively uncomplicated task, you have just experienced meditation and contemplation working together. You have also experienced a simplified version of lectio divina, a classic method of meditating on the Scriptures used by many down through the centuries. (Whole books are available on the topic!)

Other ideas for meditative moments:

SCRABBLE: Create a Scrabble-like game out of words you find in a particular psalm: Try Psalm 18 for starters. The re-mixing of the key words differently on the page leads your spirit to see them in a fresh way.

SING A NEW SONG: Create a simple song based on a word such as *alleluia* or a short scriptural phrase such as "Blessed be the name of the Lord." Sing it over and over as it leads you into deeper levels of meditation. If you play an instrument, accompany yourself with a simple repetitive chord progression.

MANTRA: A mantra is simply a spoken repetitive phrase used to aid meditation. As in the singing idea, it can be a single word, such as *alleluia* or *maranatha* (Aramaic for *Come, Lord*) or a phrase of your favorite Scripture or even a single vocal sound. As for me, my heart usually gravitates to "Blessed be the name of the Lord."

JESUS PRAYER: Many people repeat what has become known as the Jesus Prayer: "Lord Jesus Christ, Son of God, have mercy on me, a sinner."[24] The prayer originates from the Desert Fathers of the fifth century. So, fifteen centuries of people have found it a significant gateway into the meditative space.

variation 1: The phrase can be silently repeated while inhaling on "Lord Jesus Christ, Son of God" and exhaling on "have mercy on me, a sinner."

IMAGERY: Meditation can also result from visually focusing on an image or scene. This is the concept behind the use of icons in the Orthodox Church—that meditation arises from spiritually crafted iconic images. However, a similar experience can spring from other images as well, whether it be the view from your vacation getaway spot, one of the inspiring photos going viral on the Internet, or a painting in a museum or in your own home. This is the reason many classic still-life paintings included some macabre element such as a skull—so they would lead the viewer to a healthy reflection about life *and* death. (*Imagio divina*, perhaps?)

SONAR: Could there be a certain sound that could help you plumb the depths of your own soul? Of course! The sound of rain on your bedroom window, children playing in the schoolyard, crickets in the backyard on an early summer evening, a distant train horn, thunder rumbling in the heavens—these sounds among others can, at the right moment, take you into the meditative-contemplative cycle. My favorite soundscape is large church bells ringing. My meditations on these through the years have led me to four points that my own reality and desires have in common with bells:

1   Bells can touch us deeply, even viscerally. I love feeling their vibrations deep in my gut.
2   They usually announce something of importance, which is also part of my role in this world.
3   They are often out of tune,
4   And usually out of rhythm as well.

Hey, that's me! I've officially adopted the marvelous sound of massive bells ringing as my life's sound statement.

108

LABYRINTHS: I've been experimenting with labyrinths for the past decade. I find them to be an intriguing meditative device. First of all, they look pretty cool just as public artwork. Second, they are playful. If adults step out of excessively driven lives and allow their inner child to walk my labyrinth, it's been worth it for me. But third, labyrinth walking is an interactive image, an ancient yet still powerfully charged metaphor for the adventure of life. At the entrance of the labyrinth there is a decision to face—to accept the invitation of the journey or not—much like the call of the reluctant hero as in so many of our epic novels and films as well as God's call on our lives. Once within the labyrinth, there will be feelings of disorientation, of confusion, of being lost despite the fact that there is but a singular path. To many this confusion represents the difficulties and insecurities we often feel in life. At times we feel we are going nowhere or even moving away from our desired destination. At last, the journey leads to the center of the labyrinth, which can signify many things: a moment of self-realization, of finding God, of receiving strength and grace, of releasing unnecessary burdens, of experiencing peace and rest, just to name a few. Coming back out of the labyrinth, contemplative adventurers realize the experience of the journey has somehow renewed their perspective and mysteriously equipped them to re-enter society and become the humans they were created to be.

(It may help to point out the difference between a labyrinth and a maze. A maze is an intellectual problem to solve with many choices and dead-end paths. A labyrinth, on the other hand, has only one path that leads to the center. The maze is for the mind, the labyrinth for the soul. If you are fortunate enough to live near a labyrinth in a public park, then by all means, go try it out sometime—especially if you can be alone and have time for walking at a relaxed pace. If possible, incorporate a labyrinth walk occasionally into your spiritual feast.)

Sometimes I create what I call "guerrilla labyrinths," temporary labyrinthine installations in public spaces. I see it as a way to inject an intensely meaningful yet nonthreatening spiritual symbol in the midst of everyday life. Check out www.guerrillalabyrinths.com for photos of my labyrinths—indoors and outdoors, in grass, sand, stone as well as some made of snow, duct tape, garden hoses, ropes, and even strands of lights.

109

REPETITIVENESS: You may have experienced this before, but sometimes repetitive actions such as knitting, washing dishes, mowing the lawn, driving a car on the open road, rowing a kayak, or walking around the block can allow you to naturally experience a form of meditation. Have you ever seen Jews praying at the Wailing Wall? Most are swaying back and forth repeatedly. An overly simple explanation is that when the logical left side of the brain is somehow pacified with repetitive, physical action and relaxes its guard, then the spiritual and creative right side of the brain is set free to do its thing. Try it out—experiment with seeking that elusive meditative moment while performing some of your repetitive daily tasks.

Chapter 13

CONTEMPLATING

ENCOUNTERING GOD IN THE DEPTHS OF YOUR SOUL

Silence is God's first language.
—JOHN OF THE CROSS

O my divine Master, teach me this mute language
which says so many things.
—JEAN-NICHOLAS GROU

TAKE A VACATION FROM YOURSELF!

How does this idea hit you?

- Yes, please!

- What the %*&# are you talking about?

- Sounds creepy, no thanks.

- Ooooo! Tell me more . . .

- Think I'll jump to another book.

- When can I start?

P ersonally, I've found it quite refreshing to take a vacation from myself every now and then.

Suppose you found out that, due to some weird turn of events, you are (and have been) the owner of a seaside property but never knew it. They tell you that your oceanfront home has a beautiful veranda overlooking the sea. On the veranda, there's a big comfortable chair. A cool, refreshing breeze from the sea blows constantly. What you would do? The first question in my head would be, *Where is it?* Then, *How do I get there?* At the same time, I would be checking my calendar to set a departure date.

"OK," you're probably asking. *"So how does this work, this vacation from myself?"* Well, it's an interior thing—an inner journey, so to speak—it's how Father Thomas Keating humorously describes the prayer of silence that we are calling contemplation[25] (while still remembering others may call it meditation).

It may not be an oceanfront villa exactly, but there *is* indeed a beautiful sacred space within you. It's been there for some time. The Creator formed you with this inner sacred space. It's a place of extraordinary peace and tranquility—a place that has never, ever been messed up by all the other stuff that has happened in your life. A place where no other person has been before you to screw it up. A place that is for you . . . just as you need it to be . . . that fits you . . . because it is yours . . . only yours.[26] This inner sacred space is where we meet God. Jesus referred to it as the "Kingdom of God within you."[27]

Our challenge is to figure out where this place is and how to get there. Here's one clue: If you take a vacation, it usually means leaving one place behind and going to another place. So to find your inner vacation villa, you first need to leave behind, release, let go of, and cease the activity of your normal, everyday life. This is usually done by carving out some time in your schedule to be quiet and alone for a few minutes. Put everything else on hold . . . and just relax.

BE STILL AND KNOW

This is where silence comes into play. I realize extended silence seems out of place in this book, which has encouraged a smorgasbord of crazy, creative concoctions to fully engage the mind and senses. All the moments of praise and thanksgiving and confession and all the creative expressions have actually been preparing the palette and synchronizing the soul with the Divine. In these few moments of silent rest in the arms of God, something deep can happen . . . something that is beyond what words or thoughts or creative acts can express . . . something that is far deeper than the plane of rational thought . . . or "the kiss of God," to borrow a phrase from Meister Eckhart.[28]

Thomas Kelly put it this way: "The sooner we stop thinking *we* are the energetic operators of religion and discover that God is at work, as the Aggressor, the Invader, the Initiator, so much the sooner do we discover that our task is to call people to *be still and know*, listen, hearken in quiet reflection to the subtle promptings of the Divine."[29]

However, even once you find this moment of quiet, inner rest, and silence, you will quickly realize that your busy-every-moment-of-everyday brain doesn't want you to give it a break—not even for a few minutes. It immediately assaults you with a barrage of thoughts, concerns, plans, worries, dreams, etc., to let you know in no uncertain terms that even your random, wandering thoughts are very necessary and that a vacation from them is definitely *not* an option! So the more you try to relax, to be quiet, and to let go, the more vicious the brain attack.

This is where I really appreciate Cynthia Bourgeault's and Thomas Keating's style of contemplation/meditation called Centering Prayer. They accept this mental onslaught as totally normal: "If you find yourself tangled up with a thought—no matter what kind of thought—you simply, gently let that thought go. You release it, thus

113

bringing yourself back into alignment with your original intention" —to find your inner vacation villa. "Of course, the next thought may be right back, reducing the duration of your bare, formless openness to not much more than a nanosecond. But that's not the point."[30]

The point is that when each thought arises, you practice releasing it, letting go of it, and returning to your focused inner journey. Bourgeault and Keating suggest choosing a simple sacred word (like *grace*, *return*, *peace*, etc.) which will serve to signal a return to the center. Each time you release and come back to your contemplation, you are marking the trail, creating a rut in the dirt. You are training your soul to no longer be at the beck and call of your brain and its totally rational agenda. Much like walking away from your office with open files on the desk or turning off your cell phone and putting it in a drawer for a day, you *can* learn to turn off the persistent mental activity that characterizes most of our waking hours.

This can also be viewed as practicing the art of "dying to self," one of those nearly impossible-to-attain feats that Jesus assigned to us. However, I do enjoy thinking to myself sometimes, *You know, for about 15 or 20 minutes today, I can say I was very close to being dead to my-self—dead to my thoughts, my agenda, my desires, etc.* It's like taking baby steps, knowing that baby steps can eventually become grown-up steps. Cynthia Bourgeault tells us that Centering Prayer is also practic-ing *kenosis*,[31] the same concept of divine self-emptying that we find in Philippians 2. This is characteristic of the very essence of who Jesus is: his incarnation, his life, his teaching, and his death on the cross.

Let the same mind be in you that was in Christ Jesus, who, though he was in the form of God, did not regard equality with God as something to be exploited, but emptied himself, taking the form of a slave, being born in human likeness.

And being found in human form, he humbled himself and became obedient to the point of death—even death on a cross. (Philippians 2:5–8, NRSV)

115

Like many things in life, "being still and knowing" takes practice. It is counter-intuitive. Don't expect to master it the first time you try it. But try it. Trust yourself. Enter the labyrinth—it always leads to the center. Learn to listen to subtle cues from your spirit instead of the barrage coming from your brain. Practice releasing each disruptive thought. You *are* capable of finding your way. Even more importantly, you will be able to find your way back to this place whenever you need another soul-refreshing vacation. The more you beat the path down, the easier it will be to find again.

Just as the long, tiring endeavor to reach an actual vacation villa is well worth it once you are there, so is this one! You've got the rest of your life to work on it and to enjoy repeated journeys. *Bon voyage!*

FILET MIGNON: As hinted above, a few minutes of well-placed silence doesn't just fit in nicely with the other elements of a spiritual meal. We can actually consider all the other courses along with all creativity as introductory preparation for the few moments we cease talking to God and really listen to him in silence for a while. In his presence, we cease asking, doing, or even thinking; we allow ourselves to simply *be* with him. It is my hope that all the other activities and prayers included in these chapters will result ultimately in an insatiable appetite for "just being" with God.

CENTERING PRAYER: Find time in your schedule for a period of twenty minutes of straight up, hard-core, silent contemplation. As mentioned above, realize beforehand that your brain *will* barrage you with seemingly very important thoughts. This is the time to practice releasing each thought as it comes your way. See it as an exercise in holding at bay your intellect so that you can bathe your soul.

variation 1: If you find twenty minutes overwhelmingly long, start with five minutes and later work your way up in five minute increments.

variation 2: I've run across some people who have an objection to the term *centering prayer*. Instead they refer to this practice as *abiding prayer* based on John 15. Call it whatever you like. The terminology doesn't matter, the practice *does*.

DEEP CALLS TO DEEP: I love the image of Psalm 42: "Deep calls to deep in the roar of your waterfalls; all your waves and breakers have swept over me." Often while keeping periods of silence, I start by asking for the very depth of God to call out to the deepest place of my soul. Even though I don't fully understand it, I quietly say that *now . . . this moment* would be a good time for it to happen, however that happens. I also imagine the deepest part of my soul mysteriously calling out in its loudest "roar" to its Creator and waiting not for just an empty echo but for the responding roar of his mighty waterfall. It's such beautiful yet ancient imagery!

BREATHING: Richard Rohr often relates the story of how a Jewish friend helped him understand the richness of the name *YAHWEH*. He said that the two syllables actually have the sound of breathing in and then breathing out. Try it yourself. Become so still and silent that you are only aware of your breath . . . and that in your very breathing, you are repeating the most holy name of God: YAH (as you inhale) . . . WEH (as you exhale) . . . YAH . . . WEH . . . YAH . . . WEH . . .

117

    Think about it. His breathy name was the very first word you uttered at your birth, and it will be the last one just before you die. *How beautiful is that!*

CUES IN NATURE: There are many aspects of nature that underscore the importance of silent contemplation.

Variation 1: Find an inspiring outdoor spot near where you live, the kind of place you can visit regularly to sit in stillness and silence. Listen to the subtle sounds of nature you would have otherwise overlooked. Rejoice in each one.

Variation 2: As you enter into any natural environment, look for examples of release (*kenosis*) such as trees releasing their leaves each fall.

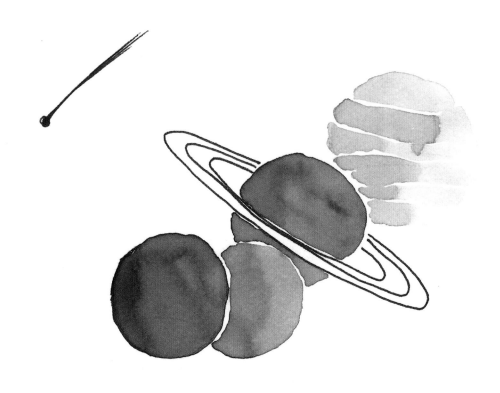

Chapter 14

ASKING

EXPRESSING YOUR NEEDS

I can picture God saying,
"Okay, hon. I'll be here when you're done with your list."
— A N N E L A M O T T , *Help, Thanks, Wow*

Ye have not, because ye ask not.
— J A M E S 4 : 2 (K J V)

I f you were to ask the average guy on the street if he prays, he would probably interpret that as inquiring whether he asks some divine force for help and expects, or at least hopes, for an answer. It seems that asking for holy help for oneself is the entry level and perhaps the only level of prayer for most people. We all find ourselves in those life-jams where there seems to be no way out and when the heart of even the most irreligious among us cries out a desperate, "Dear God, help me!" I have certainly been there.

Anne Lamott calls the prayer of "HELP!" the "first great prayer."[34] I think the next level up from that would be deal-making with God—I've been there too. You know how that one goes—"Oh God, if you will just do this one little thing for me, I promise you I will . . . "

Without a doubt, this is the hardest chapter of this book for me to write. There was a time when asking for myself was just about the *only* kind of prayer I practiced. Now I've given so much time and creativity to develop other kinds of prayer that, to be honest, I often find myself "going easy" on the basic prayer of petition.

Petition can easily become the most self-absorbed and egocentric prayer on the menu. Often, though, my own lack of asking isn't because I consider it a more primitive form of prayer or that I want to appear less selfish. The reality for me is that when I have spent a good amount of time in praise and thanks and contemplation and the others, I find that when I get around to asking for my own needs, God seems to often stop me with . . . *Yes, Dave, I know all about that situation . . . No need to even ask . . . And hey . . . I've already gotcha covered.*

Here is yet another admittedly inappropriate analogy, but allow me to share it anyway because I personally find it helpful. Within a relationship, there are many ways to get what one wants from the other person. There's the above-mentioned deal making—the *quid pro quo* thing. I suppose there's also extortion, but that would tend to bring a swift end to most relationships. Then there's the old silent treatment, which forces the other to eventually ask what's wrong. (FYI: That doesn't work very well with God since he usually *is* the silent one!) Another popular method is nagging—just keeping on bringing it up every day, multiple times a day, perhaps even more effective if you use a pitiful, whiny voice.

The best way, alas, the truly "high road" to get something from another, is to love them so much that they stay awake at night thinking up ways to love you back, to thank you, to repay the affection. I know, I know . . . God is *not at all* on the same level of our human and often petty relationships, but I feel that something like that happens in my relationship with him. When, rather than nagging, I spend more time loving and thanking him and experiencing him in the depths of my soul, I feel he's already dreaming up ways to bless me and is already one step of ahead of my requests. That said, there are clearly times we should lay out our needs to God, and we can always feel perfectly justified and comfortable in asking for his help. This is, after all, quite biblical.

The Bible is full of requests for God's help for all manner of things:

- Abraham asked for a city to be spared.

- Moses asked to see God's glory.

- Hannah asked for a son.

- Gideon asked for a sign of God's support in battle.

- David asked for God to keep his promises.

- Solomon asked for wisdom.

- Hezekiah and Jehoshaphat asked for protection.

- Nehemiah asked for success in rebuilding Jerusalem's walls.

- Job asked for answers to his many questions.

- Jeremiah asked for national restoration and renewal.

- Daniel asked for God to listen, forgive, and act.

- Jesus asked for unity among his followers.[33]

When Jesus's disciples cornered him and asked him specifically how to pray, he gave them an example we call the Lord's Prayer. This well-loved prayer asks God for a number of basics: daily bread, protection from evil, forgiveness of sins, and that God's reign and will be lived out on the earth. These categories, by the way, make a good outline for shaping some of your own prayer times.

Jesus's thoughts on the subject are also quite clear: "Ask and it shall be given to you . . . For everyone who asks, receives . . . whatever you ask for in prayer, believe that you will receive it and it shall be yours."[36] Add to that a couple of his stories where people are so persistent and obnoxious that they end up getting what they kept requesting.[37] Case closed. We are definitely encouraged to ask!

Sometimes, though, the biblical narrative records incidences when prayers were not answered as expected. The classic example is Paul's three unanswered requests for God to relieve him of the "thorn in my flesh."[38] In contrast, great blessings were bestowed that were never asked for or even imagined. Did Mary ever ask to be the virgin mother of Jesus? I doubt it.

There is one unavoidable problem with prayers of asking and even of interceding. The problem is that when we ask, we are squarely expecting the God of the universe to intervene and change circumstances in the situation. If he doesn't, we're left with that awkward, foolish, and disappointed feeling we have all probably experienced. The Christian community has created a set of trite clichés to try to explain or to help us deal with the situation: "It evidently wasn't God's will" or "God always answers prayer with yes, no, or wait" or "You just needed more faith." In my opinion, though, these explanations only serve to dig the hole deeper.

I remember a popular conference speaker humorously dealing with the inherent craziness of expecting immediate divine intervention by pretending to be a TV weatherman giving the forecast in real time as various religious groups in the region were praying about the weather. It went something like this: "As you can see we have a low pressure developing here for the weekend, so lookout for the rain . . . Oh wait, the ladies of a church are praying for clear skies for their picnic, so we're now seeing the low pressure system shift to the south . . . Oh no . . . hang on . . . now the farmers have gathered to pray for much-needed rain for their crops and the low pressure seems to be remaining in place and intensifying . . . "

I wish I had the definitive answer to unanswered prayer. I'm afraid I don't. I struggle with this dilemma just as the rest of humanity has through the ages. C. S. Lewis nails it by saying, "Every war, every famine or plague, almost every death-bed, is the monument to a petition that was not granted."[38]

When we reflect on the full narrative of the Bible, though, we observe that even the struggle of unanswered prayer itself is biblical. For example: the entire book of Job! The psalmists express this struggle in a myriad of ways:

- "How long, O Lord?"

- "Will the Lord reject his servant forever?"

- "Answer me, quickly!"

- "Are You listening?"

The eleventh chapter of the book of Hebrews, referred to by many as the "Role Call of Faith," is a litany of amazing things that happened to people because they had so much faith: Abel, Enoch, Noah, Abraham, Isaac, Jacob, Joseph, Moses, and even Rahab, the prostitute. I think we can also assume there was a petitionary prayer associated with most of them. However, have you ever noticed that the same chapter concludes with another list of people who presumably also prayed but whose prayers were definitely not answered? "Some faced jeers and flogging, and even chains and imprisonment. They were put to death by stoning; they were sawed in two; they were killed by the sword. They went about in sheepskins and goatskins, destitute, persecuted and mistreated . . . " (Hebrews 11:36–37).

Just after Jesus's ascension, his followers met with lots of prayer time to select a replacement for Judas. There were two names on the short list. They prayed that God would show them which to choose. They chose Matthias. But since we never hear much from Matthias, and especially after a guy named Paul experiences a rather dramatic conversion and moves into an important leadership role, some have said that even the apostles misread an answer to their prayer.

So if the apostles can blow it, what are *we* to do? We are definitely told to ask, but it is quite obvious that not all requests, maybe even very few, will be granted exactly as we ask. Allow me to offer some suggestions:

- Ask for less. I tend to reflect seriously on my requests before I lay them before the Father. I feel strange calling on the God of the universe, the Ancient of Days, the Great I Am, to please give me a close parking spot at the shopping mall.

- Ask with wisdom. You may be asking God for pinpoint precision when he is answering within a less precise circle. Often God, like a wise earthly father, doesn't coordinate every aspect of our lives and make every decision for us. He has given us intelligence, unique gifts, distinct life passions, and a sensitive spirit to help guide us. Through the past few decades, I have appreciated and lived by the incredible wisdom contained in the book *Decision Making and the Will of God* by Garry Friesen.[38]

- Ask according to his will. I'm not talking about some elusive, secret "Will of God" shrouded in a fog of mystery; I'm referring to God's obvious desires expressed abundantly in the Scriptures. He loves justice, peace, grace, goodness, healing, acceptance, salvation, inclusion, redemption, renewal, reconciliation . . . the list goes on and on. The will of God also follows Jesus's example of caring for the poor, the sick and the marginalized . . . his way of giving and going . . . his self-emptying and self-sacrifice . . . his creative stories about an alternative kingdom. Conversely, it would be implied that the will of God is not necessarily centered around our personal happiness, individual fulfillment, or economic abundance. But when what we ask for is in sync with the example Jesus left us—his mission to heal humanity, to restore relationships, and to spread his kingdom of love here on earth—then things can happen!

In the 1970s, before the fall of communism in Eastern Europe, Sanan and I did a little Bible smuggling into Poland. One of the "deliveries" that we were to make was to an address in a high-rise apartment on the outskirts of Warsaw. There was no designated rendezvous date or time—we just showed up. On the morning we arrived, our contact (an engineer by trade) had felt in his spirit that he should stay home from work that day. We were worried that someone may have followed us or that we would be putting him in danger if he welcomed our "gifts" and us into his home. During our conversation, he alluded to the fact that on several other occasions, he knew he had been observed carrying and distributing unusual quantities of Bibles and other suspect materials. He went on to say that actually the police could enter his home at any moment and arrest him for this illegal activity. On hearing this, I grew anxious and let out a rapid-fire stream of suggestions, schemes, alternative scenarios—anything that would help protect this precious man and his family. One of my ideas was to devote serious and concentrated prayer to this situation. After thanking us for our willingness to pray for him, though, he calmly told us this little parable: "For most of the history of humanity, people thought the earth was the center of the universe . . . that the sun and other planets revolved around the earth. But as we matured in our understanding of the cosmos, we realized that everything in our galaxy actually revolves around the *sun*." Then he simply left that thought hanging in mid-air, unprocessed and unexplained.

After some time to reflect, I realized I was in the presence of spiritual maturity way beyond my own. I was seated with a man who clearly seemed to be in the center of God's will, who was literally serving as the hands and feet of God to bless many other people with their own copy of the Bible. He had every right to ask God for protection, for intervention, and for miracles, which he probably did on a daily basis. But prayers for his own security seemed much less important to him than his prayer to follow the way of Jesus into self-sacrifice and self-emptying, to let his life truly revolve around "the Son," no matter the consequences. Needless to say, I walked away from his humble apartment that day with a cherished lifetime memory and a vision of what real spiritual maturity looked like.

So, I'd say, ask with abandon. Once you feel assured in the best wisdom you have that your request lines up with what God is all about, then ask with persistence and boldness. Ask unashamedly and unapologetically. Settle in for the long haul and keep asking. Remind God of the crazy stories that he gave us about people asking with persistence and then, just keep on asking.

Since "asking" prayer is the first form of prayer for most people and since it too often lingers on as the only prayer for many of us, the objective of this book has been to move beyond this beginning point. I want to suggest that we expand our concept of prayer so that the default definition changes from asking God for stuff and expecting him to answer, to creating space with God where a wide range of prayer happens—prayer that is less self-absorbed and more God-focused— prayer that is less egocentric and more spiraling outward toward others.

CREATIVE IDEAS?

By now, you should be able to concoct a few prayer recipes of your own for "asking" based on the examples in earlier chapters. Personally, I simply present my requests to God in a very humble, old-fashioned way—by just asking him. Very little fanfare. Very little extra creativity. It could just be me, but as I said before, when I concentrate my time and spiritual energy on other courses in the meal, I find this one needs much less elaboration.

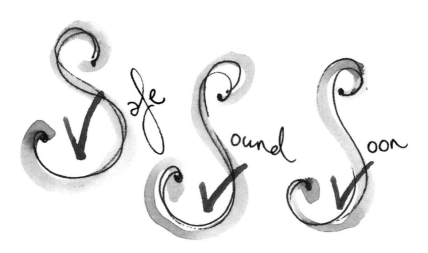

Safe Sound Soon

Chapter 15

INTERCEDING

ADVOCATING FOR THE NEEDS OF OTHERS

"Dear Jesus, do something."
—VLADIMIR NABOKOV, *Pale Fire*

If one person is praying for you, buckle up.
Things can happen.
—ANNE LAMOTT, *Help, Thanks, Wow*

uring a brief visit to Amsterdam, Willemijn invited us to a fascinating church service. She informed us that a famous local comedian was going to lead it. The event was part of an ongoing monthly series where the church opened up to hear from local celebrities regardless of their religious persuasion (or lack of it). cool idea . . . but incredibly risky! I thought. *Will the evening's comedic guest just do some kind of religiously tainted stand-up routine?*

I was more than a little surprised when she started leading the service from the very beginning: the welcome, the announcements, the hymns, etc. It was all a bit awkward since she wasn't accustomed to the church's normal religious routine, but she did know well how to turn it all into comedic material. For example, she didn't really know how to introduce and lead the hymns so she said, "Hey everybody . . . that's Hans over there on the organ. Give it up for Hans! [*Applause*] Now take it away, Hans!"

When it came to the prayer time, however, she actually became serious and proceeded by saying, "As I mentioned earlier, I'm an atheist, so I don't really pray to God. *But*, when my friends tell me their troubles, I *do* tell them I'll be thinking about them. So, I'd like for us to take a few minutes and collectively *think* about our friends who are going through rough times." And that we did! So on a certain level, probably all of us have cared about, hoped for, and interceded (in our own way) on behalf of those we care about . . . even atheist comedians. Who would have thought!

That's a good starting place for intercession, a bit like knowing how to fry an egg. But now let's take it up a notch—Eggs Benedict perhaps?

When we carve out a regular space in our menu for intercession, it brings with it some interesting dimensions.

- First, there are tons of ways to introduce creativity to the task of intercession.

- Second, intercession provides a natural way to add just a smidgen of spiritual salt in just about any secular environment, even hostile ones. The next time you're at work or a party and someone shares something about a recent difficulty or tragedy, try responding with, "You know (or maybe you didn't know but), I'm a praying kind of person. Would you mind if I pray for you and this situation during the week?" It could be slightly awkward at the moment, but it lets your friend know who to turn to when they really need prayer.

- Third, it gives a chance to have a long-term impact on somebody's life by interceding for them on a regular basis. My friend Sam Caudill in Atlanta once told me he was praying for me on a certain day every week—Wow! My wife met a humble older woman in Washington State who came up after a conference to tell her she had been praying faithfully and daily over a period of years and that it was such a pleasure to see her again. Wow, again! These kinds of prayers have a phenomenal impact.

- Fourth, it gives us the opportunity to soar way beyond our small prayer space (wherever it is) and impact the world. We can intercede for world leaders, world events, unreached people groups, and even entire nations.

- And last, but by all means not least, intercession gives us a chance to tangibly see and hear about the results of our own prayers—to see God in action. This can be quite surprising and inspiring. After all, we *are* dealing with an amazing God—"[He] who is able to do immeasurably more than all we ask or imagine, according to his power that is at work within us" (Ephesians 3:20).

Back in Rio de Janeiro decades ago, I once received the disturbing news that two members of our church had been kidnapped at gunpoint in their car while stopped at a traffic light. They were being held for a ransom—something totally unreasonable like $5 million (an all too common occurrence in Rio at that time). Even though I didn't really know this young adult brother and sister very well, I began having a strong calling to intercede on their behalf. But it was more than that.

I felt as if God was in the room with me, saying something like, "Listen Dave, I want you to be my lead guy in the prayer coverage for these two friends. I want you to bring together everything I've been revealing to you about prayer and focus it all on this situation. I realize I've never asked this of you before . . . but I think you can figure out what to do. You're my guy!"

"... Uh, me? Are you sure?"

To be honest, I didn't know where to start. But since the memory of my spiritual hunger strike was fresh in my gut, I decided to begin with fasting. That, I could do.

When the first Sunday came, I expected everything at church to be geared toward praying for the kidnapped pair. To my astonishment, it was pretty much business as usual, except for one in-depth announcement about the situation and a general reminder to pray.

This motivated me even more to seriously pray. I decided to go on a spiritual retreat for the next couple of days at a friend's mountain house. I remember my main prayer being somewhere in the realm of *"What do I do?" "How do I do this?" "Give me some ideas"* . . . or (to be more biblical) . . . *"Oh Lord, teach me to pray!"* (Luke 11:1).

One idea that came quite quickly and clearly was to mobilize friends to intercede with me. So I called a handful of church friends (young and old) who I knew were serious prayers and organized a meeting. They all showed up.

Now remember, I didn't really know what I was doing. I'd never led a prayer meeting for people being held ransom by really, really bad guys with guns that kill and who have secret hideouts. The seriousness of this life and death situation was beginning to sink in. I wanted this to be more than just "a prayer meeting as usual," so I bought several poster boards and thick markers. When my praying friends arrived, I had headings on the posters that grouped together the various "players" in the situation:

1. The kidnapped guy
2. The kidnapped girl
3. Their parents
4. The kidnappers
5. The police who were going to rescue them
6. The church and our role in prayer support

The idea was to write down our prayer requests on the poster boards and then seriously intercede for each topic using these written cues as reminders.

My own prayer at that point was simple: Rescue them safe and sound and make it soon. End of prayer. It didn't matter how it was done, by whom, just get it done. So I was really quite surprised when my friends started throwing out rather detailed requests for me to write on the posters. Here are a few that I remember: (My unspoken thoughts are in italics.)

- "I want to pray that they not be separated so they can support each other." (*Ok, good, but not essential, in my humble opinion.*)

- "Let's pray they have a Bible to read." (*Again, great idea, but what are the chances?*)

- "I'm praying that the kidnappers are kind to them." (*Wow, I'm just hoping they don't beat them to a pulp!*)

- "I really want to pray they have a chance to share their faith with the kidnappers in a way that will help them want to change their ways." (*Well, okay. Why not go ahead and ask for the moon?*)

- Then I added my simple request that they be rescued safe and sound and soon.

The ordeal, however, went on and on and on . . . days turned into weeks. I had heard disastrous accounts of similar situations where Brazilian SWAT teams entered hideouts killing everyone in sight because their main goal was to kill the bad guys, not so much to liberate the hostages. After about twenty days, all seemed hopeless to me. My faith wavered. I was out of ideas . . . and out of hope. I quit my fast. My faith was on empty. oh well, good try, Dave.

In the end though, on about the thirtieth day, my prayers were answered—they *were* rescued safe and sound, it just wasn't quite *soon* enough for me. The following Sunday, the entire church service was one big celebration of thanks. And of course, our two friends shared the entire ordeal from beginning to end. I'll never forget what happened in the pews as the story unfolded. Several of the details seemed to have a direct correlation with things that we had prayed for and had written on the poster boards. To be honest, many things I didn't think were necessary and probably wouldn't be answered— can you guess?—*were* answered! For example, the two were actually chained together. We *did* ask that they not be separated . . . check! They found a Gideon's Bible in a closet that they were able to read to each other. We *did* pray for a Bible . . . check! Each time this happened, all of us in the poster prayer group gawked around the room, catching each other's eye to make sure that we all recognized the answers to our intercession. It went on . . . the girl celebrated her birthday during the captivity, and the kidnappers actually bought her a birthday cake. So, they were fairly "nice" . . . check! The girl also shared a long conversation she had with one of her captors about her faith and how God could help him get out of this racket and really do something with his life. She said the guy had goose bumps on his arms. Meaningfully shared faith . . . check!

What did I learn from this experience? Plenty.

1   God sometimes invites us to intercede in special ways for special circumstances.

2   Friends may have way more faith or discern different things than we do, but that's why it is very often a good practice to pray together with others.

3   God is not limited by our faltering faith or how long we can fast. He invites us in on his activity even knowing we can't handle it. Fortunately, he's able to get the job done anyway.

And now . . . some recipe recommendations for your intercession course.

136

PLAYING CARDS: Index cards are a fun way to organize inter-cession for people, events, organizations, and institutions. You can go for the multicolor pack (neon or pastel) or just plain white if you prefer to doodle and color on them yourself. Putting just one name on the top of each card allows you to group them together in various ways. You can also make notes on each card of specific needs, the dates you prayed, answers to prayer, progress, etc. If you are not a particularly organized person (like me), index cards also allow you to randomize who/what you pray for. You don't necessarily have to group them by subject. You can keep things fairly haphazard and "just pick a card . . . any card" from the stack.

Variation 1: This same concept can work on your smart phone or tablet. There are apps available that work like note cards.

Variation 2: Index cards are also great for small groups. Have par-ticipants jot down one prayer request per card. Save the cards so the group will have an ongoing record of recent prayer topics. Sometimes you can scatter them randomly on the floor or table and ask people to pick one to pray for individually.

Variation 3: You could use postcards or gift cards instead of in-dex cards. If you're a "card shopper," take the time to choose beautiful post cards to represent those whom you pray for regularly. Keep track of your prayers and any progress or developments on the blank side. Scat-ter the cards around on a table with the images up to create a wonderful visual collage of intercession.

PHOTO PRAY: Intercede for friends or family by printing photos of them from your computer. Make each picture lighter or more transparent with a photo editing program. Then print it on a full size piece of paper. Write bits of your prayer (words, phrases, blessings, desires, wishes, biblical verses) all over the picture until it is full . . . all except the face of your friend.

variation 1: This works as a blessing as well—fill the page with good, purely positive things that you pray will be poured out upon your friend in the photo.

variation 2: Get even more creative—draw pictures or doodle on the page, use colored pencils, crayons, or markers, or make a collage.

variation 3: Try it with a group photo of friends or family.

variation 4: Try it with a picture of a place (office, school, home, church) or a map (city, state, province, country).

variation 5: Try it with a picture of yourself.

REALITY CHECK: Allow your own everyday realities to focus your prayer on the needs of others around you, as illustrated by this journal entry: *Dear God, today I don't feel like praying because, to be honest, my back is killing me . . . but help me to pray for those who are in more pain than me . . . I pray for those in my city in pain . . . in the hospital, in nursing homes, even students or those in business, anyone feeling the pressures of overwhelming deadlines . . . I especially pray for those in developing countries who are in pain who don't have medicine available to them . . . etc.*

137

138

BIRTHDAY PRAY: Most people keep track of the birthdays of those they love. On these special days, take a few extra moments to focus your time of intercession specifically on those who are celebrating a birthday.

Variation 1: Find a picture of them to look at while you pray.

Variation 2: Print out their picture and write/draw your prayers all around them (as above).

Variation 3: Not only pray for them, their needs, and their future, but if the relationship has been long, spend some time making a "thanksgiving list" for the shared memories, their gifts/talents, accomplishments.

Variation 4: Contact them by phone or social media, or send them a card. Include some of your memories and dreams for them and/or a well-crafted prayer or blessing.

DIVIDE AND CONQUER: Let's say you sense a desire to intercede for someone in a special way. One idea is to think through the situation and divide it into different parts based on all the people involved (like the prayers for my kidnapped friends above). For instance, if a friend's wife is very ill, who besides her also needs prayer in this situation? The wife, of course, and her husband, but also the rest of the family and friends, as well as the doctors and nurses caring for her.

Allow this fourfold structure (number can vary) to stimulate your creativity:

- Divide a page into four sections or simply use four pages and start writing. Use four different colors of ink, if you like.

- Doodle your requests on the different sections of the page. (For more on this, I highly recommend *Praying in Color: Drawing a New Path to God* by Sybil MacBeth[39] on doodling your prayers.)

- Pray in four different rooms of your apartment/house.

- Face four different walls of a room.

- Use four different body positions as you pray.

- Use four colors of poster board mounted on the wall. (Works well in a group setting, as you've seen.)

- Find four different Scripture passages and get creative with them—sing them, write them with a calligraphy pen, memorize them, etc.

- Ask three other friends to join you in prayer for four days.

- Decide on four objects that represent your prayer concerns, and place them together somewhere as a reminder. Focus on one of them each day for four days straight.

- Allow the numbers 1, 2, 3, and 4 to remind you to pray when you come across them throughout the day.

SOCIAL MEDIA: The next time a friend contacts you by e-mail, Facebook, Twitter, etc., asking you to pray for them for whatever reason, take a few moments right then and there to type out a prayer (or a blessing) in response. Recently my friend Tracy told me that her family printed out such a prayer I had written so they could re-read it from time to time.

variation 1: If you have the time and the computer skills, copy your prayer text onto an appropriate or inspiring photo/ image. Send it to your friend.

variation 2: Snap a photo of your handwritten or doodled prayer. Send it privately through social media or by e-mail.

FOLDED PAPER: Hold a plain piece of paper horizontally. Bring the side edges together to make a fold. Then fold it again in the same direction. When you open it, your paper should have four columns. If you consider both sides of the paper, you have eight columns. Label the top of the eight columns: *Everyday, Monday, Tuesday, Wednesday, Thursday, Friday, Saturday,* and *Sunday.* Now divide your prayer requests and topics of intercession in the eight columns. For example:

- Everyday: my family, close friends, certain pressing concerns

- Monday: my work, work friends, bosses

- Tuesday: national leaders, my in-laws

- Wednesday: state or provincial leaders, my sports friends

- Thursday: my kid's teachers, my art friends

- Friday: my kid's friends, recent world events

- Saturday: my neighbors and friends who need God in their life

- Sunday: my church, missionaries, and unreached people

You may keep the same paper for years (until it falls apart), or you can keep it fluid, changing it often, changing the order, color coordinating it, getting artsy with it, doodling on it until there's no more space left, or even filling each column with layers of tiny overlapping sticky notes.

COUNTING SHEEP: We've probably all tried the "counting sheep" technique of attempting to fall asleep in the middle of the night. What if you saw your neighbors, instead, and what if you prayed for each one instead of just counting? Try this: visualize your street, neighborhood, town, or apartment building. Proceed in a systematic fashion to bring each neighbor's face to mind, offering a one- or two-sentence prayer and then moving on to the next. This may be the only kind of prayer where the goal is actually to fall asleep. (Actually, it's not ever such a terrible thing to fall asleep while praying. What better way is there to enter into your night's rest than directing your last thoughts of the day toward God and others?)

YOUR TURN: Do you think you could invent a new way to pray for someone in particular? Look for elements in your everyday life that trigger a prayer for that person: colors, sounds, certain foods, a specific genre of music, etc. For long-term intercession, you could dedicate a beautiful notebook to carefully writing out your personalized prayers, doodles, designs. You may even have several notebooks for specific friends and ongoing concerns. Look for what works well for you. Use your own passion and creativity. Have at it!

MISSIO DEI

Chapter 16

JOINING

ALIGNING YOURSELF WITH GOD'S MISSION IN THE WORLD

[I]f I touch God I must touch man, for there is really no distinction.
Christ incarnated himself and became man,
so I must, like Christ himself, be a person of the towel and the water.
That is to say, wash the feet of my fellowmen as Christ did,
and washing the feet of my fellowmen means service.
—CATHERINE DE HUECK DOHERTY, *Poustinia*

elcome to the course most recently added to my spiritual menu. It is quite ancient. I'm probably just slow to catch on. Since I tend to do this course last, I envision it as a shot of *espresso* after a great meal—small but extremely potent.

The conclusion I've come to over the past few years is that the best way to conclude a good time with the Divine is by acknowledging my willingness to join him in his activity . . . to join him in his grand dream of filling the world with peace, grace, love . . . in making himself known . . . in bringing his kingdom of heaven right here to the kingdom of earth.

So, as a concluding course, I do something to establish the fact that I want to be available . . . I'm joining up . . . I'm willing to be used . . . to be sent . . . to go.

It was around 2.5 millennia ago when Isaiah set the precedent for this. He had an amazingly dramatic and sensual spiritual experience that you can read about in the sixth chapter of the biblical book with his name. In fact, his experience flowed along the same lines as the meal concept this book keeps repeatedly going on about.

- For Isaiah, it started with praise: He had a vision of God Almighty on his throne surrounded by angels who were saying to each other, "Holy, holy, holy is the Lord Almighty; the whole earth is full of his glory."

- Then, confession and reconciliation: As the angels spoke, they caused the building to shake and to be filled with smoke. Isaiah was understandably terrified and confessed aloud, "Woe to me! I am ruined! For I am a man of unclean lips, and I live among a people of unclean lips." At this point, an angel flew to him with a hot coal from the altar. When it touched his lips, his sin was forgiven and his guilt taken away.

- Now God had Isaiah's full and undivided attention. As Isaiah contemplated what had just happened, it was only necessary for God to drop a short and simple pair of questions, "Whom shall I send? And who will go for us?" These are the same questions God asks today: who will represent him and his grace to the people around the corner or around the world?

- Isaiah, hearing and wanting to join in the call of God, responded with a classic prayer, "Here am I. send me!"

In the New Testament, another equally dramatic scene unfolds in the twentieth chapter of John. Jesus had just been crucified. The revolution of love he had been leading had seemingly come to a crashing halt. His followers, to say the least, were devastated. To add insult to injury, Mary Magdalene was running about claiming to have "seen the Lord," who they knew had died and been buried. That very night, Jesus's followers fearfully gathered together and shut themselves in a locked room to try to pick up the pieces and figure out what to do next . . . when . . . (dramatic pause) . . . *the resurrected Jesus miraculously appeared in the room!*

As in the Isaiah experience, once the Eternal Word has your attention, very few actual words are needed. Jesus spoke, using just four one-syllable words to his friends, "Peace be with you." Then he showed them the crucifixion scars, and they knew it was him. Their sadness turned to overwhelming joy. Jesus repeated, "Peace be with you," adding the key phrase: "As the Father has sent me, I am sending you." Those in the room had just heard the very essence of Jesus's message. Did they really hear it? Do we really hear it?

Bottom line: *God is a sending God*. He sent Isaiah. He sent Jesus. He sent the disciples. He sent many others. He sends us! That's *the* key reason for the relationship: to be sent . . . to be his envoy . . . to become like him . . . his hands and feet in the world. Our response is simple: say *yes* . . . and *join* him.

And "join" is a great word because it implies that we will not be alone on this journey. In fact, the very next phrase that Jesus spoke to his followers in that room was, "Receive the Holy Spirit." Wow! He provided a way to enable us with his very presence, wisdom, and power.

"*MISSIO DEI*" has become a popular way of describing the vision of this God who sends. Alan Hirsch puts it this way: "By his very nature, God is a 'sent one' who takes the initiative to redeem his creation. This doctrine, known as *missio Dei*—the sending of God—is causing many to redefine their understanding of the church. Because we are the 'sent' people of God, the church is the instrument of God's mission in the world."[40]

So, as you can see, joining up with this sending God is not just a good ending for our prayer time. It's actually the *reason* for the entire prayer experience, as well as the *purpose* of Christ's body, the church.

Recently, while out walking and praying on a tree-lined Parisian boulevard, I thought of an idea allowing other kinds of praying to flow directly into the *missio Dei*. It's not really an idea, it's a phrase . . . well, not really a phrase, it's just a conjunction . . . a two-word conjunction. You probably remember from high school grammar that a conjunction serves to join two words or phrases together.

Here it is: a simple idea for adding clearer missional purpose to your prayer. When you are praying in the "asking for stuff" mode, whether it is for you or for others, try adding this little conjunction *so that* to the end of your petition, then try to express the reason for your request or the eventual desired outcome.

Once *so that* is included after your request, you begin to really ponder the *why* of your prayer. It actually forces you to reconsider and re-think what you're asking. This practice also encourages you to line up your own desires with what God desires: whatever is good, gracious, encouraging, caring, healing, inclusive, loving, peaceful, etc. —kingdom stuff.

Perhaps an absurd example will help explain: "*Dear God, uh . . . please give me a couple of million dollars . . . so that, uh . . . let's see . . . uh, so, that I could have a comfortable life, free of debt with plenty of the latest gadgets, and, uh . . . also a really cool car. Amen.*" OK . . . well, that just doesn't jive, does it? Something is terribly wrong with that kind of prayer . . . maybe just a wee bit self-absorbed? You can ask it, but I don't think God will be very excited about answering it. It just doesn't sync with his way of doing things . . . his priorities . . .

his personality . . . his mission. On the other hand, if you changed the second half: *"Dear God, please give me a couple of million dollars . . . so that . . . I could help others who are in great need to begin to live more comfortably, get themselves out of debt, and maybe even buy their first used car. Amen."* Then, yes! That starts to line up with the way Jesus lived out his life, teaching us about caring for others more than ourselves. There are still no guarantees that millions will come your way, but at least the motivation in your heart is now noble and admirable.

At this point, my advice would be to keep the second part (maybe improve on it), and change the first part as well—the actual request. So it could go something like . . . *"Hey God . . . uh, it's me again . . . since it's unlikely you will just drop a million dollars into my bank account so that I can help others . . . I would ask that you show me how to use some of the money that I do have (and maybe to spend a bit less on myself) so that I can help out these friends of mine in need and maybe even other people I don't know yet . . . and maybe you could send a little extra work my way so that I can bless another friend with something he really needs . . . . Uh, OK, that's it. Amen."*

Now this way of praying really starts to line up with God's way of doing things. This begins to flow like the river of God, to have a rhythm like the dance of God, to start moving toward the realization of God's beautiful dream, an alternative way of living, the reconciliation of all people and all of creation with himself. What has happened is that both sides of the prayer—joined by *so that*—have started to affect each other. It forces my requests as well as the reasons for them to fit into, to conform with, to blend into God's desires and activity in the world.

Since this is a new item on the menu, I haven't developed many recipes yet, but here are a few to get you started. Experiment on your own with creative ways of joining God and being sent out by the sending God.

HAND SIGNALS: I created a simple hand signal between me and my Maker. Usually at the end of my prayer time, simply to let God know again that it is my desire to join him in his mission here on earth, I stretch out both arms while interlacing my fingers, which are all still pointing forward. It's a way of illustrating with my body that I want God's mission (represented by one hand) and my mission (the other hand) to be united. Here are a few more:

Variation 1: Hand to heart and then outward.

Variation 2: First two fingers to eyes, then toward heaven, as if to say, "I'm watching for your lead."

Variation 3: Come up with even better or more personal hand signals yourself.

SING A SONG: There are several older hymns about missions and being sent. These can be rich resources as you sing or simply recite their texts, such as "So Send I You"; "Send Me, O Lord"; "Send Me"; "Here Am I, Send Me." Various faith groups have their own meaningful versions as well (e.g., "The Summons" by John Bell of the Iona community). Others texts and tunes have yet to be written. Could one of those be yours?

ISAIAH'S MANTRA: Turn the words of Isaiah into a mantra that you repeat ad infinitum as you find yourself in various places and circumstances: "Here am I. Send me."

Variation 1: Stand up and start walking around your room, your house, your block, or your neighborhood as a sign that you accept the challenge of being sent.

variation 2: Meditate on the two phrases by breathing in on "Here am I" and breathing out on "Send me."

variation 3: Try it also while considering the words of Jesus to us, "As the Father has sent me, I am sending you."

JOURNAL ON JOINING: Consider keeping a record of your adventures in joining God on his mission to heal humanity. Make a note to yourself (with the date) on the days you feel you've helped someone, encouraged someone, prayed with someone, shared your faith with someone, fed someone, or just made life a little better for someone. It can be encouraging to scan back through your random acts of kindness a few months or even years later.

variation: If you already journal or write morning pages, instead of writing multiple journals, simply highlight with a little color the paragraphs that touch on your role in *missio Dei*.

WATER WORKS: Consider using water as a physical trigger to enhance this type of attitude and prayer. Water cleanses and refreshes. Water brings life. Water always seeks the lowest place. It's an element that reminds me that I'm following the way of Jesus. In your prayer room, a bowl of water can be used in a number of ways: Dip your fingers in the water as you pray, or sprinkle the water on your head as a sign of your co-missioning. When you are out and about, let the water anywhere (in a sea, river, lake, fountain, or even your home shower) remind you of your "sent-ness."

CO-MISSIONING PRAYER: This is a beautiful example of a prayer written by Mark Berry that can be used "as is" or adapted to reflect even more directly your own desire to join God's mission of love and mercy. It affirms our shared participation in transforming the world with God, while recognizing that we are simultaneously "specks of dust" and "divine humble image-bearers." Maybe it will even inspire you to write an original prayer, poem, or reflection of your own. As you come across items like this, whether on a blog, in a worship liturgy, or elsewhere, grab a copy to keep in your recipe file.

150

CO:MISSIONING PRAYER

In the name of the divine and mysterious Trinity,
You have called us into being through love,
You have joined us to one another in love,
You have placed us in your world to love.

Grant each one of us the strength,
To carry your blessing from this place to the next.
May we be at home in any land and in any place in between,
for all the cosmos is yours.
May we, with our hopes set on shalom in the world,
live also as aliens in all lands.

May the rhythms of your creation,
be the pulse that sustains our very life.
May the lamp of your word guide our feet,
on the unsure paths of each day.
May your breathing be the wind that leads us,
across strange new oceans.

Our lives are but a flicker of a flame,
But we are kindled from your divine Spirit.
You have created us,
humble missionaries, holy wanderers,
Specs of dust and divine-image bearers.
Shadows of your creativity,
and crucibles of the spark of innovation.
We are constantly restless until we rest in you.

Grant each one of us and our community,
a deeper fullness of being and spirit,
May our faces be fuller in glory and joy,
now bearing new shape,
as we transform and supplement one another.
May that transformation bring peace, joy and love,
in the world in which you have placed us.

In the name of the Spirit who moves across the surface of the
waters, and in each beat of the human heart,
In the name of Jesus, the God-Man,
who died, rose and lives on for us,
In the name of the Creator and re-Creator,
the source of all beauty, freedom and grace.
Amen[41]

—MARK BERRY

Part
THREE

Your apron is probably good and dirty by now. Hopefully, you've picked up a few tips and have been inspired to put into practice some of the recipes.

While reading through the lists of prayer practices, you may have had thoughts like these: "I think that would work well with my prayer group" or "I could use that idea at work . . . and this one at the park . . . or that one on my upcoming vacation."

Now, welcome to Part Three. It is precisely these types of settings that will be explored in the next two chapters: "Eating on the Run" and "Dining With Friends." We'll take a look at expanding these ideas beyond the normal prayer space. To conclude, the final chapter is my bisou to you (that French way of kissing on both cheeks before leaving someone's home). I'll share one of my favorite stories and a favorite quote just because you've stuck with me till the end.

Chapter 17

EATING
ON THE RUN

If we cannot find God in the routines of home and shop,
then we will not find him at all.
—RICHARD FOSTER, *Prayer*

He prays unceasingly who combines prayer with
necessary duties and duties with prayer.
Only in this way can we find it practicable to fulfill the
commandment to pray always.
—ORIGEN, *On Prayer*

One characteristic of Western culture, which only began bubbling up in the late twentieth century, is an obsession with eating on the run. Take-out counters, drive-thru windows, fast-food everything, car cup-holders, lunch totes, snack packs, not to mention pre-packaged, dehydrated, reconstituted, and even re-engineered fake food make it all possible. Sure, there have always been family picnics and simple meals while traveling; but we have now taken things to a whole new level. We have literally made a science of it. So much so, that a cooked meal at home in an unhurried atmosphere with the whole family present is a rare event for many.

Whether we like it or not, we *are* a culture on the run, and this lifestyle can affect our spirituality. The first two parts of this book have offered help with creating rich spiritual feasts—much like a cookbook encourages you to take time to prepare delicious meals in your own home.

However, it *is* possible to take *Pray Like a Gourmet* outside of your prayer room, to let it spill over into the rest of the house, or to even take it on the road. Beginning in this chapter, you'll find several ideas that will facilitate this "spillage." You are encouraged to personalize the ideas and begin to practice them in your own circumstances or to invent new ones of your own.

I'll start with one of my favorites. It developed out of that very desire to pull the spirit of my prayer time out into my everyday world. Occasionally, my morning prayer time has been so wonderful that I just can't say "Amen" at the end. I don't want it to stop. I actually don't want to end the experience by saying the "A" word—I just can't do it. Instead, I get up slowly and make my way to the shower, the usual next step in my morning routine before going out into the real world. There, in the shower room, as the cloud of the Spirit continues to hover low around me, I turn on the hot water.

- As the steam fills the room, I gently say, "Thank you for your presence."

- As I take off my clothes, "You love me just as I am. Thank you."

- As I stand under the water, "Baptize me with your Living Water."

- As I scrub myself with the soap, "Cleanse me from my sin."

- As I wrap myself in the dry towel, "Thank you for your strong arms of love wrapped around me."

- As I dress myself, "I put on your love, your grace, your peace, your protection . . . ."

- As I spray on cologne, "May my life be a sweet fragrance unto you" or "Anoint my head with your healing oil . . . your oil of gladness today."
- As I pause with my hand on the doorknob, "Your Spirit *will remain with me* throughout this day" or "Abide in me and I in you."

Create your own prayer habits and routines to automatically trigger spiritual moments. I love the way Jan Richardson puts it: "The mundane and the miraculous are intimately intertwined."[42] Find your own miracles in the mundane activities of everyday.

REPETITION: There are a number of repetitive tasks you do around your house: washing dishes, mowing the grass, knitting, and other repetitive activities outside of the home: walking, biking, riding public transportation, driving on the open road. Many of these seemingly mundane moments can be turned into rich times of creatively spiritual reflection. Take advantage of them.

CITY POINTS: Living as I do in Paris, I cross the *Pont Royale* (the bridge between the Louvre and the Musée d'Orsay) late at night about twice a week while returning from events at the arts space where I work, Le Pavé d'Orsay. I make it a habit to pause each time at the center apex of that ancient bridge to say a few words of thanks. Often when others were walking with me, I asked them to join me in the simple routine. Similarly, when I lived in Montréal, I made a habit of interceding for that quirky city every time I went to the Mont Royal overlook, where there was a panoramic view of the city below.

Where are the inspiring points in your city? Ones that you visit often enough to include in a habitual routine? Your list could very well include some of the worst places in town as well. Resolve to leave a prayer or blessing each time you pass one of your personal prayer "hotspots."

MINI MEDITATIONS: This is how I refer to the act of attentively pausing during the day to acknowledge beauty, goodness, kindness when they seem to just reach and grab your attention. I call these moments in-between-meal snacks that *should* be encouraged. Recently, Sanan and I were driving through the English countryside with our friends Kate and Diane. Whether they knew it or not, they both had the wonderful habit of processing their instant reactions to beauty aloud. "Oh, just look at that! I love that point where the greenest part of the grass meets the bluest part of the sky . . . and just the right variety of trees to create added interest . . . and only a cloud or two in the sky . . . Isn't it all so beautiful?" After they repeated similar observations throughout the day, I thought to myself, *Kate and Diane are helping me experience "mini meditations" when I would have normally overlooked these small, inspiring details.* I once made an actual comment about the similar habit of another friend, Lynn. She responded, "I'm just practicing the spiritual discipline of saying what is beautiful, good, and true out loud. It's a neglected art." Touché!

PRAYERWALKING: This is a great way to intercede for your neighborhood or city. I find it very creative, spontaneous, and improvisatory. It's really quite simple: just start walking, then let what you see shape what you pray for and how you pray. If you walk past a school, pray for the school kids, teachers, staff, and educational policy makers. If you walk past a clinic or hospital, pray for the sick in your community and for those who give them care. If you walk past a sports field, pray for the kids learning important life lessons through sports and the older players and coaches who are setting examples for the community. When you pass by government offices, pray for political leaders and those who keep essential services going day after day. When you pass a poster advertising a concert, pray for the musicians and the cultural scene of your city. If you notice a syringe in the gutter, pray for those struggling with addictions. If you pass someone asking for a handout, perhaps you should first give some money and then pray for that person and the many caught in the poverty spiral. I enjoy doing this kind of walk with a friend. It allows us to carry on a natural "prayer conversation" with our eyes open while each of us pick up different cues along the way. My friend Randy Sprinkle has written an excellent book, *Follow Me: Becoming a Lifestyle Prayerwalker,*[43] if you want to investigate this practice further.

UNDERWATER MEDITATION: Swimming laps in your local pool would be one of those repetitive actions that can allow your spirit to soar. Perhaps less frequently available but even more inspiring would be an occasional snorkeling experience. A friend who scuba dives regularly once told me, "Dave, you haven't worshipped until you've sensed the presence of the Creator in his underwater world."

NATURAL HOT SPOTS: As I mentioned earlier, one year I decided to connect my spirituality with various natural elements: water, stone, earth, sky, fire, snow, mountain, trees, sun, stars. I assigned each of the elements to a different month (or season). It enabled me to focus for an extended period of time on a variety of scriptures, writings, quotes, songs, and prayers that touched on each particular element. It also allowed time to get out of the house and intentionally create moments of personal worship where the element was present: a forest, mountaintop, campfire, night under the stars, wading through a river, walking in the snow, etc. The focus also impacted my creative expression in a visceral way because I always had a specific physical theme to be thinking and praying about creatively.

variation: Adapt these and other themes for your family or group of spiritual friends. Themes can easily spawn some fun group outings, road trips, or even extended retreats and vacations.

A TINY, TINY PRAYER: With some time to kill while waiting in a public place, I take a pen and draw two horizontal lines on the back of a receipt, dividing it into three equal parts. In the top space, I pick the first kind of prayer that pops into my head—for instance, PRAISE. Within the rather tiny space, I start writing in a stream-of-consciousness style, letting whatever wants to come out to do just that. I write it very tiny and dense for two reasons: (1) so no one around me can read it and (2) because my scrap of paper is *really* small. When I fill up that section, I move to the next space. On that occasion when I wrote Praise, I then chose Thanks, again discreetly writing down the first things that came to mind: people, new ideas, friends overcoming problems. Again when I filled up the space, my time of thanksgiving was over. Then I moved to the final bit of space on my paper. My mind jumped to the fact that I really wanted to continue to Join the *missio Dei*, God's mission of redemption here and now on the earth. So I randomly scribbled more tiny words, expressing this intense desire. *Et voilà* . . . a quick and simple way to "eat on the run." Give this a try the next time you're waiting for an appointment, riding public transportation, or waiting for a friend at a café.

TRIGGERS: Once I was praying for a friend who loved all things flamenco. In order to trigger prayers for him throughout the day, I allowed everything remotely Spanish—like guitar music in stores, publicity about town, and even just the color red—to remind me to intercede for him. Other friends would, of course, generate entirely different sets of prayer triggers.

AWKWARD BLESSINGS: We are all familiar with those awkward moments when we come into close proximity with complete strangers: in elevators, grocery store lines, on public transportation. Counteract the weirdness of the moment by doing something even weirder: silently pray a blessing on them. Even complete strangers may give you cues concerning their needs: obvious health issues, the kids they care for, fatigue, stress, frustrations.

SWEATY PRAYER: My daughter Kori suggested I include the kind of prayer she experiences often as a modern dancer. She encourages people to get engaged in something that involves physical activity (dance, yoga, Pilates, Zumba, martial arts, running) and set your intention beforehand to offer that time as an offering to God. Then recognize your effort and even your sweat as a physical manifestation of your spiritual worship, allowing your body to express what words cannot. (Side note: Ancient Greeks used to bottle up the sweat of their best athletes because they considered it sacred.)

FASTING: This is an ancient idea for taking prayer on the road. Everywhere you go, all throughout the day, fasting calls to mind and allows you to "feel in your gut" the gravity of your prayer concern.

Chapter 18

DINING WITH FRIENDS

Friendship is the wine of life.
—EDWARD YOUNG, *The Complaint*

When you're learning to cook like a gourmet, you eventually reach the point when you want to share your experiments with friends. You invite trusted friends over for the most elegant meal you can create. The same is true when you're learning to *pray* like a gourmet. The more you practice the ideas in this book and begin to create some of your own, the more you will realize that many of them would work well—or best—with a group. I encourage you to look for ways to share prayer experiences with friends.

GROUP LITANIES: If you have a regular group of friends you pray with, may I suggest you try a group version of the idea I call *litanies* in the Praising chapter. Basically, it is the repetition of short phrases: "God, you are _____." (Fill the blank with an adjective about God.) Or "Lord, your name is _____." (Use one of the names of God.) The phrases should be said aloud but *very gently and with a pause between them* to allow time for contemplating the words, their significance, and their implications. When done in a group who really understand the power found in this simple exercise, the result can be quite moving, inspiring, and even overwhelming. It is possible to do this so well that it essentially morphs into collective improvisational spiritual poetry as the group learns to build on each other's phrases with associations, alliterations, rhymes, synonyms, or antonyms. It naturally takes some time to become comfortable with such spontaneous, interactive group prayer. For that reason, newcomers may prefer to just listen and observe for the first time or two.

NOISY PLACES: One afternoon, Sanan and I were in a very noisy *café parisien*. We had hoped to have a simple time of prayer along with our coffee. Normally we would do this by just keeping our eyes open, seemingly having a "normal conversation" but actually voicing prayers for family and friends, as if God were sitting at the table drinking coffee with us. However, because of the noise level this particular day, I pulled out a piece of paper and drew a stick figure and assigned it a name. Sanan picked up that it was a way to pray for this person. She drew the money symbol beside my stick figure. I nodded recognizing it as a prayer that our stick figure friend would have enough money to finish school. And so it went on—more stick figures and symbols along with an occasional word or phrase thrown into the mix.

> variation: This also works well with four to six people around a table as long as they can all see the paper and participate by adding their drawn prayers.

PICNIC OBSERVATIONS: Groups of "pray-ers" can join together for many of the ideas in the Observing chapter. Invite some friends to a picnic on a warm summer day in a beautiful setting. After a time to catch up with each other and enjoy some picnic food, invite them to reflect together on just one of the natural elements that is in plain sight: a tree, a stream, the sky, the grass, the flowers, etc. What can they observe about the element? What are some parallels for our lives? If it could talk, what would it tell us? You may need to allow some time for reflection and encourage them to keep digging deeper, until inevitably, even more insightful observations begin to flow.

> variation: Add a moment of Communion to the picnic experience by bringing bread and wine and sharing a moment of remembrance together.

SYMBOLIC TABLE: If you're having spiritual friends over, try using symbolic elements as a source of inspiration. Place on the coffee table a piece of bread, a stone, a candle, and a bowl of water. Allow the symbols to set the agenda for the gathering by contemplating each element, one by one, for a few moments.

- The bread represents eating together—anything from a snack to a full meal. You have come together as friends sharing your food and your lives. This is a natural aspect of gatherings, but taking the time to reflect on and truly appreciate it as a gift goes a step further.

- The candle symbolizes inspiration. This could be a reading from the Scriptures, other inspiring texts or a short time of group *lectio divina*. You may also ask for volunteers to share an inspiring moment they have had recently.

- The stone stands for things that weigh us down. Pass the stone around the circle of friends. As each person feels the weight of the stone in his or her own hand, it is a reminder to release or share the weights of worry, stress, injustice, and sin. If appropriate, prayer needs may be shared and participants may pray aloud or silently for each other.

- The bowl of water reminds us of Jesus washing his followers' feet and leads to the question, "How are we joining him in his work?" Water cleanses and gives life. Water also seeks the lowest place and brings refreshment to others, just as we, like him, are called to do. Some participants may choose to share ways they have recently joined in God's activity. Remember, even the small things like smiles or noticing a friend's sadness are totally "what Jesus would do."

Variation 1: Add other symbols sometimes to create variety. For example, a potted plant. Let the dirt represent confession and the plant our areas of growth, learning, or development.

Variation 2: There are a great many creative ways to use symbols to provoke refreshing ideas. Consider rocks, for example:

- Take a rock, let it represent something that is weighing you down, now give it to the person next to you. Individuals may or may not choose to share the specifics of their request. Either way, carry your friend's burden in the form of the rock this week wherever you go. Then bring it back next week.

- Take a rock, let it represent something that is weighing you down. Now place it on a bandana or scarf spread on the table or floor. Once everyone has contributed a weight, notice together that if each person helps lift an edge of the bandana, the burden is lighter for all.

- Take a rock, let it represent something that is weighing you down; then drop it into a tall, sturdy vase of water. Savor the feeling of releasing your burden into God's hands.

- Let a rock represent a major problem in the world today . . .

- . . . or a burden a friend is carrying . . .

- . . . or a burden you have carried since childhood . . .

- Another option: Pile the rocks into a mini altar or simple structure and then spend time together in silent prayer for each other's burdens.

(Thanks go to Chriszine Backhouse who helped elaborate these and other ideas in our Montréal curieux community.)

PAPER CHAIN: Give each member of the group a strip of colored paper. Encourage each person to write a one-line thank you prayer. Fasten all the strips together to make a festive paper chain that can be hung across the meeting room. If you have a small group, you may even want to give each person several strips of paper. You may also choose to add to the chain week by week. The "thank you" prayer chain is particularly effective on special occasions like Christmas, Easter, and church anniversaries when a long chain can be made during a multigenerational service.[44]

NATURALLY INDOORS: Often with a group, it is not possible to get out in nature together to observe and be inspired by its beauty. You may need to invent ways to bring nature indoors, such as my experience with dragging a large tree branch inside and letting it represent a tree (from the Observing chapter). Other ideas:

- Ask everyone to bring a piece of fruit; then lay them all out on the coffee table. Ask what there is to learn from observing the various shapes, colors, and textures. Another option is to enjoy slices of the fresh fruit as you contemplate together what it has to tell us.

- There may be a great view of the sky, a forest, a mountain, or even a cityscape through a large window where you meet.

- Bring "forest fragments" such as bark, pinecones, leaves, roots, and acorns. Ask all to reflect on them and the ways they speak to or parallel our own spirituality.

- You could also use amazing photographs or videos of certain nature scenes to inspire the sharing of observations, thoughts, and prayers.

MUSICIAN-LESS WORSHIP: A friend complained to me one summer that he had to lead the service at his church the following weekend, and he already knew that all the musicians would be on vacation. I responded with "That would be great!" Surprised, and knowing I was a musician, he asked me what I would do. I suggested various ways to create an entirely music-free worship service that can work well with groups of almost any size:

- Praise by inviting people one by one to call out names of God: Jehovah, the Almighty, the Alpha and Omega, the Ancient of Days, etc. (also works for characteristics of God: good, powerful, loving, forgiving, etc.).

- Thank by each person turning to a neighbor and expressing their thanks for something.

- Confess by reading a confession in unison.

- Ask and intercede by inviting each person to write down his or her requests on small papers provided. Gather the papers together, and offer a collective prayer for the needs represented.

- Meditate on Scripture with a short *lectio* experience instead of the traditional sermon. This could also be done by breaking into small groups.

- Bless each other in groups of two by repeating a prepared blessing. Receiving a blessing from a friend or even a stranger does something for the weary soul.

- Join God in his mission by joining hands as a group and saying together a few times, "Here we are. Send us!"

I'm confident you can come up with even better and more personalized ideas for your context than these very basic ones.

170

ALT.WORSHIP: It is also possible to create meaningful worship that is not necessarily led from the front and that does not even start nor end at fixed times. Many have been experimenting with the idea of creating worship spaces where people explore a variety of installations at their own pace, much like perusing an art gallery. The first time I tried this years ago, a visitor (who later became a good friend) gave this feedback, "Thanks for letting me pray without words. It's just what I needed." Since there are already a number of great books and websites on this subject, I refer you to them:

- *Sacred Space: A Hands-On Guide to Creating Multisensory Worship Experiences for Youth Ministry* by Dan Kimball and Lilly Lewin

- *Curating Worship* by Jonny Baker

- *Creative Prayer: A Collection of Contemplative Prayer Stations* along with the website www.creativeprayer.com by Faith McCloud

Chapter 19

CLEARING THE TABLE

I accept God into me in knowing; I go into God in loving.
—MEISTER ECKHART

The function of prayer is not to influence God,
but rather to change the nature of the one who prays.
—SØREN KIERKEGAARD, *Purity of Heart IS to Will One Thing*

ENDINGS

The ending of an elegant meal. The ending of a wonderful prayer. The ending of an inspiring book. You may remember that I don't like saying "Amen," and now I realize I don't like concluding chapters either. A book is a finite set of pages. This one will be over in just a few more words. You can be assured, though, that prayer is unbounded, undetermined, and untethered. We may end a certain series of spoken words, but the spirit of the prayer stays with us, walks out the door and down the street with us. At any moment of the day, we can pop back into that same spirit with just a pause on a bridge, the thought of a friend, or the whispered word, "thanks."

Unlike a book stuck within a rigid structure of text, printed pages, and a binding, prayer, like the grace of God, is new every morning. The way we pray can morph itself to our emotions. It adapts itself to our agenda. It flows into our real-world, here-and-now realities. It blows through shut windows, locked doors, and closed countries. It elevates us to a life lived at a new level. It clothes us with loving-kindness and compassion as well as a form of humanity beyond our capability. It constantly drips love into our veins. It nourishes our souls like nothing else.

A FISHY STORY

Allow me to run the risk of boring you with just one more personal story. Another favorite place of mine to pray in Montréal was the *Musée plein air de Lachine*. It's among Canada's largest open-air museums. It is actually a large grassy park in the shape of a long triangle with a wide walking path all the way around. Scattered about in the middle are twenty or so large modern sculptures crafted by many celebrated sculptors. The shape of the park is due to the fact that it is on the point of land that divides the St. Lawrence River from the Lachine Canal (completed in 1825 to allow boats to continue upriver and avoid the shallow rapids in that part of the river.)

I spent many days (sunny, rainy, and snowy ones) walking around and around that triangle, praying. Sometimes I was mad at God and the rest of the world. At other times, I was full of the Spirit and could hardly contain the joy. It seemed to be a place always rich in metaphor: a refuge in the shadow of the city, a mighty river, fascinating modern art, families picnicking, lovers embracing, children learning to ride bikes, and on and on. I formally declared it as *my* personal sacred space (although I did concede to let others enjoy it as well.)

On one beautiful summer day, I invited Sanan to accompany me to *my* park. I happened to be in the middle of reading *Hero with a Thousand Faces* by Joseph Campbell, an amazing book that was actually the inspiration behind George Lucas's *Star Wars* films. I read quotes from the book, and we discussed them as we walked. Soon, as we sat down on the rocks at the point that divides the river from the canal, I made a concluding statement that inspiring metaphor is all along the "hero's" journey. I looked up and said, "That's why I love this park because metaphor is everywhere." As if on cue, we heard a sudden loud splash of what was evidently a large fish out in the river. Of course, by the time we looked in that direction, it was back in the water. As we continued to scan the river, just as we hoped—another large fish jumped right out of the water before us. She even seemed to give a little extra twist in the air to reflect a glimmer of sunlight. She flicked her fins the best she could. Her mouth was open to take in air, but after only a few seconds, she was back down in the water again.

After an initial "WOW!" uttered simultaneously by both of us, I said, "So, you see, metaphor *is* everywhere!" After a long pause, my wife responded with, "Okay, what's the metaphor?"

"What's the metaphor! The metaphor is . . . uh . . . it's that . . . uh . . ." I had just backed myself into a metaphorical corner. Now I had to produce! I was racking my metaphorical brain, but it was slow in delivering its cleverness. Of course, there's a message in a typical salmon jumping into the air as she swims upstream . . . but what is it?

I delayed a little longer by staring out into the river while my mind fleshed out the enigmatic message a bit more.

Finally, I said, "Okay, I'm improvising here, but this is what I've got. A fish lives in a world of water. She's perfectly comfortable there. Her gills are magnificently adapted to the water world. She was born into water, and she'll probably die in the water. But, every now and then, she longs for a different world. She knows it exists. She's seen it. All fish deep inside know it exists—a world of another dimension with practically limitless possibilities, not bounded by the banks of rivers or the shores of oceans.

"The deep longing of the fish provides her with the urge and the energy to take the occasional leap out of her world of water and into the world of air, if only for a few seconds at a time. It's exhilarating, energizing, inspiring. In these brief moments, she's allowed to dream of breathing the air, of flapping wings instead of fins, of sporting soft feathers instead of hard scales, and of soaring with winds instead of flowing with currents.

"However, she is well aware of her reality. If she tried to permanently live in that world, she wouldn't be able to handle it. She would die. Still, the longing remains. She tries to make each leap as high and as long as possible. With each one comes a shimmy and a shimmer . . . a flick and a flap . . . a pose . . . a smile . . . maybe even a fishy form of sheer joy."

As I continued to reflect, I had more thoughts: *The fish carries on with life, acquainted with both worlds. One of them she doesn't fully know or understand yet, but that doesn't hinder her from piecing together wonderful moments of joy and inspiration from her brief visits to the other.*

We, too, long for another world that we know exists. Our visits there are also all too brief, but they bring us extraordinary moments that are exhilarating . . . energizing . . . .and inspiring.

"Not bad!" Sanan replied.

DUAL REALITIES

Quaker author Thomas Kelly puts it this way:

Once [we] discover this glorious secret, this new dimension of life, we no longer live merely in time but we live also in the Eternal. The world of time is no longer the sole reality of which we are aware. A second Reality hovers, quickens, quivers, stirs, energizes us, breaks in upon us and in love embraces us, together with all things, within Himself. We live our lives at two levels simultaneously, the level of time and the level of the Timeless. They form one sequence, with a fluctuating border between them. Sometimes the glorious Eternal is in the ascendancy, but still we are aware of our daily temporal routine. Sometimes the clouds settle low and we are chiefly in the world of time, yet we are haunted by a smaller sense of Presence, in the margin of consciousness.

But, fluctuating in predominance though the two levels be, such a discovery of an Eternal Life and Love breaking in, nay, always there, but we were too preoccupied to notice it, makes life glorious and new."[47]

Count on God knocking on the doors of time. God is the Seeker, and not we alone; He is anxious to swell out our time-nows into Eternal Now by filling them with a sense of Presence.[47]

Yes! So start counting on God knocking on your door and offering you opportunities to jump into his world. Hopefully, you're now more prepared to say yes to his invitations. Imagine the look on his face when you say to him, "I've been expecting you and I've prepared an elegant feast just for the two of us. I want to truly savor our time together. You see, I'm learning to pray like a gourmet."

Please, *stay in touch* through the blog: www.praylikeagourmet.com, or on Twitter @PrayLikeGourmet.

There you'll find:

- New creative prayer recipes

- Recommended resources

- Ideas and stories from others

- Inspirational thoughts

- Great quotes on prayer

177

NOTES

1 Aired August 21, 2004 - 21:00. Transcript, http://transcripts.cnn.com /TRANSCRIPTS/0408/21/lkl.00.html.

2 I'm pleased to announce that Paul has been on a very long, epic journey in Asia that has greatly impacted his taste buds.

3 George Ritzer, The McDonaldization of Society (Los Angeles: Pine Forge Press, 1993).

4 Jeanne Guyon, Experiencing the Depths of Jesus Christ (Sargent, GA: Seed Sowers, 1975) 7, 10–11.

5 See http://www.faithandworship.com/prayers/.

6 Richard Foster, *Celebration of Discipline: The Path to Spiritual Growth* (San Francisco: Harper Collins, 1998).

7 Evelyn Underhill, *Mysticism: A Study in Nature and Development of Spiritual Consciousness* (New York: Penguin Books, 1963).

8 Peter Lord, *Hearing God* (Grand Rapids: Baker Publishing Group, 1988).

9 *La noche oscura del alma*" or "The Dark Night of the Soul" is the title of a poem by sixteenth-century mystic John of the Cross.

10 See Matthew 14:14–21; Matthew 15:29–39; Mark 6:30–44; Mark 8:1–13; Luke 9:10–17; John 6:1–14.

11 Richard J. Foster, *Prayer: Finding the Heart's True Home* (San Francisco: Harper's 1992), 87.

12 *Liminality* is a term used by anthropologist Arnold van Gennep to explain the transition that occurs in young people during tribal rituals. It is also used more broadly to refer to changes that occur during struggle and disorientation.

13 Doug Pagitt and Kathryn Prill, *BodyPrayer: The Posture of Intimacy with God* (Colorado Springs: WaterBrook Press, 2005).

14 Sarah Ban Breathnach, *Simple Abundance: A Daybook of Comfort and Joy* (New York: Warner Books, Inc. 1995).

15 Genesis 12:10–20 and Genesis 20:1–18

16 Julia Cameron, *The Artist's Way: A Spiritual Path to Higher Creativity* (Los Angeles: J. P. Tarcher, 1992).

17 George G. Hunter III, *The Celtic Way of Evangelism: How Christianity Can Reach the West . . . AGAIN* (Nashville: Abington Press, 2000).

18 Thomas Cahill, *How the Irish Saved Civilization: The Untold Story of Ireland's Heroic Role from the Fall of Rome to Rise of Medieval Europe* (New York: Doubleday, 1995).

19 John O'Donohue, *To Bless the Space Between Us: A Book of Blessings* (New York: Doubleday 2008), xv.

20 Richard Foster, *Prayer: Finding the Heart's True Home* (San Francisco: Harper One, 1992), 87–88.

21 http://cachecache-experience.com

22 I am very appreciative of Cynthia Bourgeault who has helped me to understand this beautiful interplay of meditation and contemplation. I highly recommend her book *Centering Prayer and Inner Awakening* (Lanham, MD: Cowley Publications, 2004).

23 Charles Haddon Spurgeon, *Morning and Evening* (New Kensington, PA: Whitaker House, 2001), October 12, morning.

24 Other variations of the prayer have appeared throughout the centuries:
    Lord Jesus Christ, Son of God, have mercy on me.
    Lord Jesus Christ, have mercy on me.
    Jesus, have mercy.
    Lord Jesus Christ, Son of God, have mercy on us.
    Lord Jesus Christ, Son of the living God, have mercy on me, a sinner.

25 Cynthia Bourgeault, *Centering Prayer and Inner Awakening* (Lanham, MD: Cowley Publications, 2004), 19.

26 John O'Donohue, elaborating on Meister Eckhart, said it this way during his August 2006 talk at the Greenbelt Festival in Cheltenham, England: "So, there's a place within you where no one has ever got to—or damaged, and that's the ground of your soul. There in that place, you have confidence, complete poise, courage, elegance and complete tranquility. No psychiatrist can ever know where healing comes from or when it might begin. I think it begins from this sacred place within us. And so I would see prayer as visiting at this ground within us. And I would also see love as the affinity and the belonging of these two grounds together."

27 See Luke 17:21 (KJ21): "Neither shall they say, 'Lo, it is here!' or 'Lo, it is there!' For behold, the *Kingdom of God is within you*" (emphasis added).

28 Meister Eckhart, *Meister Eckhart: The Essential Sermons, Commentaries, Treatises, and Defense* (New York: Paulist Press, 1981), 8, 205.

29 Thomas R. Kelly, *A Testament of Devotion* (New York: Harper & Brothers, 1941), 97.

30 Bourgeault, *Centering Prayer and Inner Awakening*, 23.

31 Ibid., 87–88.

32 Anne Lamott, *Help, Thanks, Wow: The Three Essential Prayers* (London: Hodder & Stoughton, 2013), 15.

33 Abraham—Genesis 18:16–33; Moses—Exodus 33:12–23; Hannah—1 Samuel 1:9–20; Gideon—Judges 6:34–38; David—2 Samuel 7:18–29;

Solomon—1 Kings 3:4–9; Hezekiah—2 Kings 19:14–19; Jehoshaphat—2 Chronicles 20:1–12; Nehemiah—Nehemiah 1:4–11; Job—Job 3:11–26, etc.; Jeremiah—Lamentations 5:20–21; Daniel—Daniel 9:19; Jesus—John 17:23.

34 See Matthew 7:7, Luke 11:9, Mark 11:24.

35 See Luke 11:5–13, Luke 18:1-9, Matthew 7:7–11.

36 See 2 Corinthians 12:7.

37 C. S. Lewis, *Letters to Malcolm: Chiefly on Prayer* (San Diego, CA: Harcourt, Inc., 1992), 58.

38 Garry Friesen, *Decision Making and the Will of God* (Colorado Springs: Multnomah, 2004).

39 Sybil MacBeth, *Praying in Color: Drawing a New Path to God* (Brewster, MA: Paraclete Press).

40 Alan Hirsch, "Defining Missional," *Leadership Journal,* Fall 2008, http://www.christianitytoday.com/le/2008/fall/17.20.html.

41 Mark Berry, Community Mission Facilitator for the Church Mission Society and Pioneer leader of Safespace community Telford in England (used with permission). http://pioneer.cms-uk.org/2012/06/19/co-missioning-prayer/.

42 Jan Richardson, from The Painted Prayerbook, http://paintedprayerbook.com/2008/03/07/#.U6MLdo1dW6w.

43 Randy Sprinkle, *Follow Me: Becoming a Lifestyle Prayerwalker* (Birmingham, AL: New Hope Publishers, 2001).

44 See http://www.creativeprayer.com for many other ideas.

45 Thomas R. Kelly, *A Testament of Devotion* (New York: Harper & Brothers, 1941), 91–92.

46 Ibid., 97.

NOTE: The websites cited in these notes were accessed on February 16, 2015.

ABOUT PARACLETE PRESS

Who We Are

Paraclete Press is a publisher of books, recordings, and DVDs on Christian spirituality. Our publishing represents a full expression of Christian belief and practice—from Catholic to Evangelical, from Protestant to Orthodox.

We are the publishing arm of the Community of Jesus, an ecumenical monastic community in the Benedictine tradition. As such, we are uniquely positioned in the marketplace without connection to a large corporation and with informal relationships to many branches and denominations of faith.

What We Are Doing

Paraclete Press   Paraclete publishes books that show the richness and depth of what it means to be Christian. Although Benedictine spirituality is at the heart of all that we do, we publish books that reflect the Christian experience across many cultures, time periods, and houses of worship. We publish books that nourish the vibrant life of the church and its people.

We have several different series, including the best-selling Paraclete Essentials and Paraclete Giants series of classic texts in contemporary English; Voices from the Monastery—men and women monastics writing about living a spiritual life today; award-winning poetry; best-selling gift books for children on the occasions of baptism and first communion; and the Active Prayer Series that brings creativity and liveliness to any life of prayer.

Mount Tabor   Paraclete's newest series, Mount Tabor Books, focuses on liturgical worship, art and art history, ecumenism, and the first millennium church; and was created in conjunction with the Mount Tabor Ecumenical Centre for Art and Spirituality in Barga, Italy.

Paraclete Recordings   From Gregorian chant to contemporary American choral works, our recordings celebrate the best of sacred choral music composed through the centuries that create a space for heaven and earth to intersect. Paraclete Recordings is the record label representing the internationally acclaimed choir Gloriæ Dei Cantores, praised for their "rapt and fathomless spiritual intensity" by *American Record Guide*; the Gloriæ Dei Cantores Schola, specializing in the study and performance of Gregorian chant; and the other instrumental artists of the Gloriæ Dei Artes Foundation.

Paraclete Press is also privileged to be the exclusive North American distributor of the recordings of the Monastic Choir of St. Peter's Abbey in Solesmes, France, long considered to be a leading authority on Gregorian chant.

Paraclete Video   Our DVDs offer spiritual help, healing, and biblical guidance for a broad range of life issues including grief and loss, marriage, forgiveness, facing death, bullying, addictions, Alzheimer's, and spiritual formation.

Learn more about us at our website:
www.paracletepress.com
or phone us toll-free at 1.800.451.5006

SCAN
TO
READ
MORE

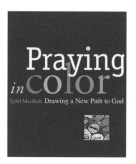

Praying in Color
Drawing a New Path to God
Sybil MacBeth
ISBN: 978-1-55725-512-9
$17.99, Paperback

Maybe you hunger to know God better. Maybe you love color. Maybe you are a visual learner, a distractible soul, or a word-weary pray-er. Perhaps you struggle with a short attention span or a restless body. This new prayer form can take as little or as much time as you have, from 15 minutes to a weekend retreat.

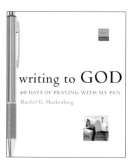

Writing to God
40 Days of Praying with My Pen
ISBN: 978-1-55725-879-3
$15.99, Paperback

If you love to write, or if you need to spark your creativity, this book is for you. *Writing to God* offers forty insightful days of prayer and personal reflection with poems and thoughts to prompt your own prayers.

> "Praying by writing takes a prayer out of my head and makes praying a whole-body exercise: my creativity is sparked, my spirit fully focused, my muscles employed, my awareness of breath heightened. I felt more connected to prayer than I had ever experienced before."
> —RACHEL HACKENBERG

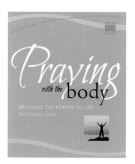

Praying with the Body
Bringing the Psalms to Life
ISBN: 978-1-55725-589-1
$18.99, Paperback

While most books about prayer are meant to be read, this one is an invitation to move in prayer by expressing the Psalms with motion. This creative approach will take you beyond your "head" into your entire being, as a way of expanding your relationship with God. Roy DeLeon has guided others in this active prayer practice for years and provides helpful drawings, Scripture texts, and explanations.

Available from most booksellers or through Paraclete Press:
www.paracletepress.com | 1-800-451-5006
Try your local bookstore first.